When Lightning Strikes a Hummingbird is a true mythic story of a man who listens to his inner voice, who dreams with awareness, and who writes a part of the mythic unfoldment of which we are all participants. Beholding Inner Earth, elves and gnomes, and pathways to a new world through personal change, the reader can glimpse a reality that is dimensionally interfaced with our more ordinary life, which is constantly changing.

The wholeheartedness with which Foster Perry faces his emotional reactions and the sincerity with which he responds to his visions and lives them opens up trials and teachings that can enlighten. Here is a wealth of stories, visions, anecdotes, and teachings that can guide the reader through her or his own transformations, where life becomes more transparent. The high-frequency energy of the hummingbird is a rare gift for us all in these times of transition.

—Rowena Pattee Kryder, author of the *Gaia Matrix Oracle* and founder of the Creative Harmonics Institute in Mount Shasta, California

WHEN LIGHTNING STRIKES
A HUMMINGBIRD

WHEN LIGHTNING STRIKES A HUMMINGBIRD

THE AWAKENING OF
A HEALER

FOSTER PERRY

INTRODUCED BY ═══════
BARBARA HAND CLOW

BEAR & COMPANY
PUBLISHING
SANTA FE, NEW MEXICO

LIBRARY OF CONGRESS CATALOGING-IN-PUBLICATION DATA
Perry, Foster, 1960-
    When lightning strikes a hummingbird : the awakening of a
healer / Foster Perry ; foreword by Barbara Hand Clow.
        p.   cm.
    Includes bibliographical references.
    ISBN 1-879181-10-X
    1. Perry, Foster, 1960-   . 2. Occultists—United States—
Biography. 3. Healers—United States—Biography. I. Title.
BF1408.2.P466A3   1993
133'.092—dc20
[B]   93-10285
                                                                    CIP

Copyright © 1993 by Foster Perry

Bear & Company, Inc.
Santa Fe, NM 87504-2860

Cover & interior design: Angela Werneke
Author photos: Daniel McCulloch © 1993
Editing: Brandt Morgan
Typography: Andresen Graphic Services
Printed in the United States of America by BookCrafters, Inc.

1   3   5   7   9   8   6   4   2

*To the ancient and living spirit
of the hummingbird,
who opens the joy in our hearts
as we become our future
on the path of the Beauty Way,
and to my parents,
Gerald and Aliki Ypsilanti-Perry.*

CONTENTS

*F*irst, I want to acknowledge Barbara and Gerry Clow for their inspiration and encouragement during the entire process of writing this book. I also wish to acknowledge Merit and Dori Bennett and Grant and Talia Kosh for their nurturing, love, and guidance while I was writing.

Special thanks also to Dawn Eagle Woman for her persistent depth of truth, to Brandt Morgan for his detailed editing, and to all those people at Bear & Company who greatly assisted in refining this book, especially Barbara Doern Drew, Angela Werneke, and Jody Winters.

Thanks as well to all the clients who came to Santa Fe for the healing and renewal of their souls. Without you, this book would not be a reality.

My dear friends Margaret Buendia-Lee, Ingmari Lamy, Joanna Moore, Michael Stuno, Daniel McCulloch (for his beautiful photographs), Peter Sterling, Diana Vivante, Joseph and Linda Lancaster, Sanda and Frank Jasper, Zena Whitcomb Kosel, Rowena Pattee Kryder, Dorothy Compinsky, Amea Meade, Leslie Christopher, Radha Baum, Barbara Hero, Carlo Castiglione, Mano Matthews, John and Lynn Pearce, K.D. Kagel, Raghu Markus, Parvati Markus, Cynthia Jurs, Mirtala, Dr. Hazel Parcells, Elaine Simard, Edith Wallace, Clyde Reid, Nilo Lucas, M.J. Sawyer, my Brazilian family—Antonio Duncan, Zulma Reyo, Gerson Carrera, Renato Gonda, and Carmen Baltestero—and all my friends in Durango, Colorado—thank you for your support and for being part of a conscious community.

Thank you, storytellers, singers, dancers, and artists

of the soul who have been my source of divine inspiration. Thank you, unseen guides, helpers, and muses who have so compassionately helped to shape and direct my life. Thanks to the angels, elves, and fairies who fill my imagination and to the elders and indigenous peoples who teach and ground me. I am grateful to be a human being in service to life. Thank you for letting me write.

Tell the people that the hummingbirds and the lightning path are coming," said Dawn Eagle Woman, Foster Perry's soul friend and a medicine woman from Wyoming. He asked her, "What is hummingbird medicine?" and she answered, "The consciousness of the dark made light, the joy that eludes humankind. It is the story of how to walk out of time's clothing in ecstasy."

When Lightning Strikes a Hummingbird is Foster Perry's experience on the edge of the Dreamtime, where parallel zones of reality interfuse everyday life. Just as the wings of a hummingbird become diaphanous when the tiny bird is poised in the air as it sucks the nectar of flowers, Foster's breathless journey in this book actually causes readers to feel their lack of solidity. Simply reading it helps us to access the high-flying vibration of the hummingbird.

The introduction of this intense oscillation by Foster into our times heralds the reemergence of a very ancient Mayan wisdom teaching. According to my Mayan teachers, hummingbird medicine is to return at this time and it will be an essential source of male healing in the late twentieth century. During the end of the Mayan Great Cycle that completes the Fourth World—the twenty years from about 1993 through 2012—the vibration of our planet is to intensify to the level of hummingbird frequency. These momentous days are to be a time of personal consciousness quickening in the midst of rapid planetary oscillation. We will *feel* our inner emptiness and penetrate the solidity and density that keeps us from vibrating at a more spiritual level. Then, once not trapped in solid definitions of self, we will be able to imagine "how to walk out of time's clothing in ecstasy."

The density resulting from patriarchal patterns does not make this faster energy oscillation during this cycle easy for us to assimilate. Foster reminds us that hummingbirds come to us when we have reached the point where we can go no further into density. At that crucial juncture, he says, the first path for males is dismemberment. This is a path that most men refuse. And so the Mayans and many indigenous people have warned that this personal quickening is our only possible salvation at the end of this particular cycle because the planet will quicken whether we do or not. We have to remember how to *adapt* to the natural energy field of Earth. This encrustation of the patriarchy creates great resistance and fear in our male sides about being willing to let go and simply dissolve. This kind of dissolving is very female, and it necessitates letting go of obsessions with personal control. So it is that the rapid wing movements of the hummingbird seeking nectar are the ideal model for male quickening at this time. That is why the Mayans chose this image thousands of years ago as the ideal one for male evolution at the end of the Fourth World.

The only way we can even exist in the face of today's planetary ecological crisis, which compromises our immune systems now that the planet cannot absorb any more abuse, is to resurrect and embody our own natural healing powers. Once we heal ourselves, we will be able to begin to heal the larger pain of the Earth. We must find a way to care enough to attend to the damages wrought by many generations who lost connection with the planetary heart; we must become passionate about our home again. Foster is a passionate man

who teaches us about inner healing. He exemplifies living for
ecstatic communion, existing only to feel the real beauty,
moment by moment, on our planet. It is living any other
way than this that creates illness and has caused us to reach
our present impasse.

According to many ancient Mayan esoteric beliefs,
Alcyone is the central star of the Pleiadian star system, and
our sun is the outermost star of this system. The Mayan
Great Cycle is a calendar that delineates the twenty-six-
thousand-year-long orbit of our sun and solar system around
Alcyone. According to the latest discoveries in astronomy,
our sun is moving into a "photon belt," or belt of light particles. As we move deeper and deeper into this photon belt,
it would seem that we are moving into the Age of Light
described in many ancient prophecies as well as by the
Mayans. My latest theory about the photon belt, which com-
bines science, astrology, esoteric sources, and secret information given to me by indigenous people, is that we cyclically
travel through this belt of light for two thousand years and
then travel outside of it for about eleven thousand years.

Because Alcyone is in the center of this Pleiadian system,
this star basks in this light field eternally. When our solar
system moves through this belt, there is always a full communion with Alcyone and the entire Pleiadian system.
When this occurs, there is a great quickening in our solar
system and on Earth. Though we do not yet understand how
this increase in photons is influencing us, it is becoming
obvious that quickening and accelerating our consciousness
could turn out to be a survival need. This new form of
increasing light seems to be mutating our bodies, emotions,
minds, and souls. Foster Perry's book contains major keys for

intentionally mutating ourselves as we move deeper and deeper into this photon belt.

I intuit that when we are in the photon belt, we are in communion with Alcyone, which then puts us into connection with the whole galaxy. When we are out of the belt, as we have been since about 9000 B.C., we are not "plugged in," so to speak, to galactic or cosmic energy fields. According to Mayan shaman and daykeeper Hunbatz Men, the center of the Milky Way Galaxy is our source, our creator. This powerful source, which must vibrate very fast, is accessible to us only by feelings, and many people seem to sense this; they are actively clearing negative feelings and emotional body blocks as quickly and thoroughly as they can at this time. Many sense that our habitual slow, dense, and stubborn feeling patterns could be dangerous in the years to come. I am sure those blocks are the source of all disease. Exactly like being able to have a mystical vision, we will be able to feel our connection with that great central source only if our feelings are pure. Clear intention coming from pure heart will end up being the basis of the next stage of our evolution.

We must clarify these negative feelings now, or we will become dysfunctional and weak in the midst of the high-oscillation frequency of the photon belt. We can quicken ourselves by vibrating at a higher frequency, and the real key to this skill is *sound*, as I will discuss later. Foster gifts us generously by showing how being struck by lightning quickened his frequency, causing him to vibrate like a hummingbird. Foster says males must become impregnated by the divine sun through surrender to the female side. Hunbatz Men teaches exactly the same idea.

When women give birth, we experience in our bodies the

quickening of the infant's soul as it enters this world. Our female parts of self know this multidimensional flash of light very well. Women have also known for a long time that most men have lost their memory of how to quicken their own vibration. This loss has saddened us, for it has created a cultural violence and ugliness that has caused female energy to retire and wait for a better time. Since this is a skill that will be needed for survival during this next phase of the cycle of our sun, I know that men are very afraid of the future. As a woman, I have looked for a male teacher who could instruct men about this frequency quickening, and Foster Perry is such a teacher. When the Earth and Sun last traveled through the photon belt around 9000 to 11,000 B.C., the Earth experienced a mini-Ice Age. Geological records indicate that during previous cycles of Earth traveling in the photon belt, there have been great climatic shifts, even pole shifts, and the comings and goings of many species. Women, who birth, have cellular memory of many journeys on this planet in millions of different forms. Men desperately need to remember their inner female so they can access these cellular records, too.

As a person who happens to be female living in these times, I also am amazed at how my male side always struggles to control. In the face of impending massive change, it struggles to hold reality as it always has been. It is in that trigger resistance that evolutionary leaps are missed and the ecstasy inherent in chaos is not imprinted. The urge to always have life instead of death, stability instead of change, causes us to be fearful instead of brave during critical leap times. We then abort a line of experience instead of discover how to mutate to a new level.

The center of the Earth is totally protected while we have our experiences on the surface. As Foster puts it, "At the center of the Earth is a silence that can contain everything. It is woven of all our feelings, stories, and memories." Finally we have arrived at the glorious moment in the cycles when our male side will also imprint this truth. However, it is our male side that has contained the energy of Earth by creating language, and hidden in that language are the sound codes of the multidimensional creative imprint.

As a healer, Foster has mastered an ancient Egyptian science called Ren, which involves using a person's name to discover an aspect of their soul. According to this teaching, our fifth-dimensional self, our soul, which is beyond duality and form, is carried in our name in this dimension. Lifetime after lifetime, our soul identity is reborn through sound by means of our names. When Foster heals, he works with name vibration through sound by singing a song of one's name. This song is the sound expression of our beingness from the source, and once heard, the sound calls our soul right into this dimension, and we begin to vibrate at the rate of our soul frequency. This method of memory quickening is a hint of the universal sound alteration to come when our solar system moves completely into the photon belt, as it will at the end of 2012, the completion of the Mayan calendar.

According to my calculations, Earth traveled in the photon belt from the last week in January until the end of the first week in May 1993. Each year until 2012, Earth's time in the photon belt will increase by one week before the entrance and one week after the exit of the year before. The Sun will move into the photon belt in 1998 or 1999, at which time

the Earth will be in it for more than half the year. When
the Sun moves in, the quickening by light will envelop the
entire Solar System, and it will be audible. (Perhaps this
is the fabled music of the spheres.)

In 2012, we will enter the Fifth World, or Fifth Sun,
according to many indigenous calendars, and this new world
is to be the Age of Flowers, an age when, like the hummingbird, we will be nourished by flower nectar. From this rich
imagery, which is already thousands of years old, it would
seem that we are about to discover new identities as hummingbirds in symbiosis with these delicate and passionate
plants. Flowers are the erotic expression of plants, and
in their nectar we taste the sweetness of the communion
of all life-forms existing when our system is traveling the
photon belt.

Foster sees the way of the future as the male/female harmoniously married, and this insight is in deep synchronicity
with basic photon physics. Until 1962, when astronauts first
detected the photon belt, physicists described photons as
occasional particles that come instantly into manifestation
when an antiparticle appears, followed by its positive analog;
they merge and—poof!—a photon is created. Beyond
physics, this is a physical expression of a universal energy
law: when a negative appears, its positive side instantly man-
ifests in response, and they merge, creating an energy field
that has no charge outside itself—it is simply energy. These
photons are activating harmonic union resulting from polarity resolution! This continual increase of photons in our solar
system will create an age of fusion instead of fission, of merging instead of duality. It would seem that the human coun-

terpart to this would be in our ability to fully develop both
our male and female sides, so that the divine marriage, the
hieros gamos, becomes our existential self.

So, as a female as far as my body is concerned, I am
excited about this book because I feel it offers wisdom for the
female's current antiparticles: our male sides. In the simple
life of this healer and shaman, Foster Perry, there is an ecstatic strength that can challenge our male sides into a deep
examination. I know Foster well, and he lives very much in
the moment in a swirling field of multidimensional *eros.* He
has learned how to bring the knowledge existing in other
dimensions to his clients.

Foster gave a powerful healing to my oldest friend, who
had lost her husband and could not tolerate this reality without him. Speaking of the Egyptian knowledge of Ren, her
name is Hope. With classic shamanic power, he went into
my friend's consciousness and found that place in her where
this dear mate still lives, eternally, for their divine marriage
is beyond time. Foster helped her remember the numinosity
and creativity of real love, and so she did not become lost in a
universe of mirrors with no images left to be seen by her. In
this book, in which Foster talks about how he experiences
reality, there is no personal Foster Perry. This is an egoless
book that exposes the vital force of this one man, and this
exposure offers truth about our own real capacities that very
few of us dare to imagine we could ever reclaim.

We will quicken to the pace of the hummingbirds during the next twenty years. We will be struck by the lightning
that moves from the sky into the core of the Earth. We can
resist this cosmic party and choose not to attend, or we can
begin laughing now and intensify our frequencies by remem-

bering all the parts of ourselves that we think once existed in other places and times. When these great cycles culminate, all the parts of ourselves miraculously fuse. All we have to do is dissolve and yet stay in our bodies for now. Welcome to this deep dive into hummingbird medicine to be able to vibrate with the frequency of the coming Fifth World, the Age of Flowers.

Barbara Hand Clow
Santa Fe, New Mexico
May 1993

Barbara Hand Clow is the author of Chiron: Rainbow Bridge Between the Inner and Outer Planets, The Mind Chronicles trilogy, *and* Liquid Light of Sex: Understanding Your Key Life Passages.

I have always felt a powerful connection to
the forest. My first name, Foster, is short for "forester," one
versed in the science of planting and taking care of forests.
My last name, Perry, alludes to pear trees, and when I first
moved to Santa Fe, I planted a pear tree in the front yard,
taking infinite care of it. On the front door of my home there
is a plaque with an inscription that reads: "Story of the trees'
house, caretaker of the forest's soul." As a child, all my memories are of what I call the "violet forest"—the treetops turning a violet color at dusk. The night turned the forest into a
violet rug, stretched over my body to keep my child spirit
warm and protected. I searched for owls in the night air, feeling safe to explore the darkness and chaos of my wild soul.

This book is the tale of my search for my soul and the
soul of the world. To understand why I am alive and how
to be fully alive, I wanted to name my roots, origins, depths.
I wanted to meet the Beloved, the Self. Clients always ask,
"When did you begin your work?" or "Where were you
born?" I am passionately Greek, East Indian, Spanish, Por-
tuguese, and Irish, and this is an autobiography of how I
came to hear the passion play of my soul and feel at home in
the world.

Though I am a storyteller, I have kept the events of this
book secret until now, not sharing the gold of experience
before it was digested. It is time to share all my pain as
love—the ungroundedness of youth, the clichés of New Age
crystals and channeling, the shadow of violence and naïveté,
the ego's isolation and loneliness, the coming to terms with

my parents and family, my rebirth. Since I wrote this book, my parents and I have felt closer and more intimate, as if a great weight has been lifted and resolved. This book has transformed me.

No one really heals anyone else. Healing comes through us when we are an empty vehicle. To do service aids us in transforming our own souls. In a recent near-death experience, I left my body and reviewed my life from another perspective. I did not remember what I had accomplished in this life, my ambitions or successes. I only remembered and reviewed the quality of my loving and the quality of the love I had received from others. All we remember after dying is the shared communion of our souls, the empathy. Empathy, the opening of the heart to feel and enjoy another as oneself, is the reason we are alive and interdependent on Earth. Knowing what another person feels, beyond ourselves and our limited perspectives, is why we live.

Mindfulness is the practice I use to slow down and see the world as it is. Eating slowly, walking gently on the ground, experiencing every breath, sensation, and nuance of thought with an inner smile—all these are the practice of mindfulness. Many clients who are HIV positive have worked with me to learn the techniques of being in the body, feeling and loving each breath and each movement of skin, in order to recreate and enhance their lives through conscious breathing. Over several months, people who at first came to me confused and distraught learned to relax, breathing attentively through their pain to the other side of it, seeing colors in the landscape for the first time, perceiving the ecstasy of simplicity in nature. Many gradually became HIV negative, well on their way to a new life of disciplined awareness. Patience, the gradual work of cherishing the body and soul, is difficult.

It requires trust, endurance, cooperation, and holding to the belief that we are innately good.

No one is inherently bad, no matter what they do or how they feel inside. No one is defective, and no person is greater or lesser than we are. We are all equal because we come from the same essence. Surrendering to love is surrendering to our essential self. Life is a mirror of accepting, without judgment, the different masks of our essence.

When the personality surrenders to the soul, then we are uniquely connected to the Self, which is God, a reality much greater than our limited perspective. Life is a sacrifice of the personality, the limited perspective, to a greater reality, which is unconscious in us. We are here to make God conscious, to help God feel creation. We are creative stewards of a new Earth.

The practice of living passionately requires discernment and listening. The teachings of this book involve listening to the etymology of words; listening to our dreams, myths, fairy tales; noticing the sacred geometry in nature, the archetypal processes in and outside our psyches, the human body. We can hear the lost treasure of our souls. I hear life as the voices of spirits, ancestors, the spirit of the land, the inner voices of animals, the sound of objects. I discern images and meanings and listen for their combinations.

I walk lightly on the Earth to hear the communication of distant voices. We are not separate from anything or anyone. We can breathe in another's pain and breathe out trust, kindness, and love. However, when we are identified solely with our personalities, we feel alone and long for communion with the Self. It is through embracing our aloneness and the ensuing chaos that we reconnect with humanity and become creative agents of the Self.

I connect to my clients' souls through literature. Before I work with people, I read them poetry—by Rainer Maria Rilke, Rumi, Lalla, Anthony Machado, Pablo Neruda, W.S. Merwin—or a good passage from Marion Woodman's work or *Women Who Run With the Wolves* by Clarissa Pinkola Estés. I also sing, chant, and intone to express every emotion I can feel inside them, mirroring back the density of their feelings. I empathize with their inner wild children and return them to the forest.

This book is the story of the first thirty-three years of my life and how I began to howl. I howled for the thickness of the ancient past. I wanted to find the hidden jewels I was missing in the busyness of living.

In the violet forest, I used to look for bleeding heart flowers (*Dicentra spectabilis*). I would lie on the dirt floor of the forest, which was filled with nettles and pine cones, and look up into the flowers, into the face of my bleeding, grieving heart, and see that it was as beautiful as this flower. I felt the heart of the world crying, bleeding, and decided then to follow the path of the medicine person. Magnolia trees, mimosas, evergreens, elderberry trees, pines, flax, poppyseed, cicadas—I feel safe in a world where nature is bold, magnificent, diverse, and powerful.

This book is a tool to weave us back into the thick forest of real self-discovery, real creativity. I hope you are moved, enchanted, filled. That was my intention in sharing these hummingbird medicine stories with you.

WHEN LIGHTNING
STRIKES A
HUMMINGBIRD

PART ONE

BEGINNINGS

LIGHTNING STRIKES

Raven, Raven,
Teach me the way
to the blue hummingbirds . . .

*R*aven came bearing gifts of the Dream-
time, dropping feathers from her wings. Day after day, magical feathers dropped from Grandfather Sky onto my head or
onto the path right in front of me. I shapeshifted into Raven,
groomed my tail, and talked to the Ancient Ones from inside the Great Mystery as they sent my body long-distance
healing. They called me by my medicine name, When Lightning Strikes a Hummingbird, and said, "Tell your story,
that others may tell theirs. Live your joy, that others may
know love."

I held fragile little bodies of hummingbirds in my hands
as I wrote the pages of this book. They died to remind me to
live my life in joy and grace and to extract the sweetest elixirs
from every experience to share with you. I thought to myself,
If God can keep his eye on a sparrow—or, for that matter, a
raven—then I must belong in this universe.

You see, the Earth is a cosmic egg that sent out a message for one sperm to impregnate it. That chosen one was you. She loved you so much that she called out for you to enter her womb. She knew your soul before your parents did. Millions of other souls never made it here. You belong to the Earth and are never alone in her care. She is a large, sentient being calling out to you, her lover, so make love to her in all your actions. We come here like hummingbirds, to sing a vibration of pure ecstasy, to fly in any direction, to create more love by opening our heart feathers, to suck the nectar of every flower. That is our birthright.

I had to be hit by lightning to know the Earth's love. I had to learn there was nothing more important in this universe than to discover how to love every sentient being. That is the story I have to tell. I was hit by lightning under a trembling sky in an open field and did not die; instead, I had the sweetest taste of kundalini that changed and sped up my life like the wingbeats of a hummingbird.

In New York City, on March 12, 1985, I was struck by lightning. As I lay on the ground, my whole body began to shake and vibrate. Electricity pulsed through my cells like a great clearing of everything I thought I knew, followed by rain and more rain. I heard strange sounds, like radio waves whooshing in my inner ear. Then my head became filled with a deep, persistent humming. It was the humming sound of the heart opening, as when the Fifth World of the Maya opens to visions of Ghost Dances and Sundances and for one brief second the world is not dual but one, perfect in every image.

Later on I learned that this experience was my shamanic initiation, but back then I thought I was crazy. I kept seeing a hummingbird hovering in front of my third eye. What did

it want? Then a burst of opalescent, iridescent colors flooded
my senses: orange-pink, silvery blue-green—colors I had
never seen before. I tasted something sweet—the nectar of
the pineal gland opening into pure bliss. There was this persistent humming, and I felt worlds cracking and my spine
splitting in two under the weight of false structures of reality, shattering under a lightning spell. My light body was
igniting. The nectar of the pineal gland was quenching years
of spiritual thirst. Boundaries between time and space, physical and nonphysical, were dissolving.

Why me? I wondered. Why the lightning path of Cauac,
the initiation by fire? It was because I was mostly "water"
and approached my experiences emotionally. I needed the
"firewater," an alchemy that makes you drunk on life.

I saw a vision then of a diamond, like my body joining in
a sacred marriage with the center of the Earth, like a magnet
drawing me to it. I was radiating electricity from the lightning bolt and being sucked into the core of the Earth—to
fit inside it somehow, to impregnate it. I saw medicine men
chanting, doing the Ghost Dance, dancing like animals. I
had to remember these songs, I kept telling myself, because
I would use them to help others heal their souls and return
them to their bodies.

My body was turning a deep purple, and I kept hearing
the number nineteen . . . nineteen . . . nineteen—the end
of karma, the beginning and the end. Suddenly I could feel
the carbon memory of my body turn into a diamond shape,
resonating in ever-widening rings of being. I was in ecstasy,
discovering the sun, the Atoma, in the center of the Earth
and merging with it.

I started to have flashes of where I had come from, far
from Earth . . . Alcyone in the Pleiades and Alpha Centauri,

our closest stellar neighbor. Then I was shown a star map, the actual pathway I took to get here as a spirit. I knew I would have to recreate this map in a weaving or carpet and sit on it and meditate. I knew I could always return to this moment at will. . . . Sirius, Venus . . . Venus was brought to this solar system on a comet's tail. It does not revolve in the same direction as the other planets. It is a very different place—home of the Kumaras, East Indian spirit beings—a place with rose-quartz buildings, plumed archways, and twin souls deciding whether or not to make the journey to Earth.

Did I believe all this? Outside of time, I could contemplate and believe everything forever and ever. I chose just to stay in the experience, hoping I would survive it without becoming insane. I knew I had prepared for this in other lives and that I was somehow entitled to this moment. I immediately longed for everyone I knew to experience the same thing.

I began to dream of yurts, domes, pentagonal buildings in communities. I saw people living in circular, curvaceous dwellings, growing crops in spirals with many new ceremonies for each season. People were equipped with organic computers to transmit thoughts over great distances or record dreams through the nerve endings in their hands. I saw children dancing and playing who were happy to be alive—children loved by both their parents, communicating through "telempathy," a mixture of thought and feeling.

I was amazed at Inner Earth. I saw tunnels, then maps of underground tunnel systems with portals in the Andes, the Amazon, Easter Island—all over the planet. I saw other-dimensional scorpions and jackals guarding these entrances to make sure people did not venture into Inner Earth unprepared.

I began to think about the wrathful deities of the
Tibetan Buddhists and the devils and demons of Chris-
tianity. I even tried to conjure them up and face them, but
they never materialized. I saw the Earth as a pristine Eden,
untouched by humans, a place where animals went in the
Dreamtime. Had I entered into the Dreamtime of the
Aborigines?

I saw white handprints on cave walls. I felt the Earth
breathing through these caves. I breathed uranium from
inside the Earth through my cave lungs at sacred sites
guarded by the Lakota and Hopi in North America, the
Aborigines in Australia, the Maori in New Zealand, the
Dogon in Africa, the kahunas in Hawaii, and the shamans
of Siberia. I felt a deep connection to the red people, the
Keepers of Traditions, and to the red earth. The pulsing
veins of my bloodlines were the ley lines of the planet,
electromagnetic waves of earth meeting sky.

In my vision I saw how ley lines converge in places of
intense initiation. I saw etheric temples not yet physically
present on Earth, each marked by different rays of color.
These were rejuvenation centers where people went to
remember who they were and had visions of star codes and
rainbow bodies—like the feathered serpent, Quetzalcoatl,
recognizing himself in all human beings.

Then I saw artists building obelisks, columns, and altars
at the crossings of the ley lines. At first only lone individuals
appeared, then hundreds of people came to construct large-
scale outdoor projects, carving mandalas and figures and
"watchers" in the faces of the red rocks all over the world.
People began to gather and sing in twelve-tone harmonic
scales, their overtones resounding through the air. Human
beings stood in hexagonal webs, the seed modules of crea-

tion, making tones as they got closer and closer to the center.

Jacob's Ladders—standing columnar waves—were created wherever people gathered to commune with Mother Earth. I saw that these people were enacting a ritual transformation of DNA from the two-strand to the twelve-strand helix. Like strands of pearls reaching for the sky, people were waking up to multidimensional living. Food looked different. There was blue food, and enlightened children had set up centers of teaching.

New ley lines crossed like synapses in the planetary brain. Where once there had been churches honoring Saint Michael and Mary Magdalene, now there were new monuments—often impressions of animals in the landscape—to show where the ley lines had shifted. The zodiac was being imprinted onto hills, fields, and mountains like the shadow of a huge cloud. I saw rainbows as full circles being completed inside the Earth and people building boats to navigate these arcs.

Then I saw the past. I saw the Earth being created, with galactic matter spiraling around it. I saw the Earth as a primordial egg of earth, water, air, and fire, then as matter, time, space, and spirit. I had a vision of the weave of the ancient Celts, the Web of Wyrd, the web of all life. The continents were all one. Everything was possible then. Four great rivers from that time still remain inside the Earth, and we intuitively navigate them in our waking dreams.

First, I discovered, was the land of Pan, also called Pangaea, a real world of mythological figures including satyrs, nymphs, centaurs, griffins, elves, fairies, devas, brownies, gnomes, and angels. They sang life into existence, as in J.R.R. Tolkien's novel *The Silmarillion*. With the help of Sirius, large Elohim angels created a vast network of energy

to hold the vibrations of Earth intact and to record every
thought and feeling of every sentient being that ever existed.
Every soul memory was sent through Jupiter to a huge, central diamond complex on Alcyone in the Pleiades.

During that time, the archetypes were being formed on
Earth. Totems, seed syllables—the whole world—were created from color and sound, from one thought, desire, and
intention. Souls were created through constellation material
mixed with Earth matter, and each soul had a frequency sig-
nature pulsing in its heart that could be monitored for its
development and evolution.

I saw a huge diamond coming to Earth and being
received—a diamond that had originated in the Pleiades. I
saw how at one time Lyrans, Sirians, and many other extraterrestrials had colonized the Earth, leaving their memories
and genes behind for hybridization. Comets, lightning
storms, and polar shifts had also periodically affected the
Earth.

I saw the first matriarchies in Lemuria, the Motherland.
There were twelve tribes of women, in an enclave separate
from the men, doing healing work. I saw the first matriarchy
of Atlantis during a golden age. I even saw that Long Island,
where I grew up in this life, was once an ancient training
ground for the Atlantean priesthoods and that Sedona in
Arizona, Bimini in the Bahamas, and even Texas were once
beds of an ancient civilization like that of the later Anasazi.

I saw that the Atlanteans had three major cataclysms,
two natural and one humanmade. That period was a time of
much extraterrestrial diplomacy, with spaceships going back
and forth. Many of these ships were organic, as though the
vessels themselves were living beings.

The last destruction of Atlantis came at a time when

extraterrestrials wanted to speed up the evolution of the planet in order to control it. The urge to dominate and control the indigenous peoples was being perpetuated by beings from outside the Earth. When I saw this, my heart felt a deep pain, which I share with all people and all races. It was the wound of being human, the shadows of our ancestors murmuring in our blood for justice and resolution of conflict.

Approximately ten thousand years ago, a major electromagnetic cataclysm occurred that altered our DNA and forever made us fear power. People sought to control nature with logos, or technical knowledge, and to create a myth of the stronger over the weaker. I saw animals change and become fierce mirrors of humans. Matriarchies gave way to patriarchies. The histories of the twelve tribes of Israel, which originally had women's names, were rewritten as the histories of the male clans.

Those in the Nile region constructed male lineages, and this practice spread all over the world. The Sumerians altered human DNA, mined minerals in Lake Titicaca and South Africa, and colonized Iraq. In Nippur, Iraq, the oppressors constructed a great temple intended to enslave other human beings by altering their genetic codes.

All these people had forgotten how to feel, how to resonate with the core of the Earth. They were technologically advanced, especially in metallurgy, but they lacked feeling and heart. Their matter was inert. Their central sun was dying.

I was fascinated by visions of India. I saw how the north had enslaved the south through invasions. Dravidian India was taken over by the Aryans, their hunter sky-god religion mixing with coastal, earth-centered agricultural communities in the south. I saw Krishna and the blue-skinned people, living and teaching in the high Himalayas as part of a tribe. They came down from the mountains to communicate and interbreed with other races of varying skin colors. At that time, Earth was truly a rainbow planet, mirroring the multi-colored spirits that were created at the beginning of time.

Eventually, the Rama empire of India created incredible weapons and attacked Atlantis. The *Ramayana* and the *Mahabharata,* the epic books of ancient Hindu mythology, are the records of what today is called the Third World of the Hopi and the Maya. The Maya had lived all over the world, keeping accurate records of planetary cycles, remembering the Sacred Hoop of all life.

Then a dream of the Americas uniting flashed before me. The Himalayan energies moved back to their source in the Andes. Rivers connected, continents joined, circles were completed. I saw the chakras, the fiery energetic pinwheels of North and South America, light up. Belize was the crown chakra of its local region, Costa Rica the heart center. The ancient pathways from Chile to Alaska would be joined in 1992. We had all come back home to where we first incarnated on the planet.

When the atom was split, we all started returning en masse from the stars, as though in answer to a sharp siren. We came back here to do ceremony, to hold the balance of creation through love and clear perception, and to witness our own rebirth and the rebirth of the Earth.

In A.D. 2013, we will come to the end of a twenty-six-thousand-year cycle. That will be the end of time as we've known it. Now we are in alignment with the Great Central Sun of creation, and millions of other planets are in that same beam. This is the birth of the Fifth World, the world of the hummingbird.

Grandmothers and grandfathers held me as I, a man, became pregnant with the Earth and gave birth. The divine child that emerged from me was a new man, differentiated yet androgynous, his male and female sides harmoniously married. My body went through all the pain of giving birth, as well as all my past lives and the accumulated rage, anger, and tears. I was completely dismembered. This was my initiation into true humanity.

Then I saw black-and-white butterflies and a large black Sun Lodge where the Keepers of the Webs of the Earth had gathered. There, Raven, Dolphin, Elk, Frog, Armadillo, Bear, and Owl introduced themselves as my allies, and finally I heard a humming in my left ear.

"You've been lying on the ground for hours," said my friend Peter, who had come with me to the field and had been walking nearby. "What did you see?"

"Did you see the lightning?" I asked him.

"No," he answered. Peter had seen nothing.

ELVES

*A*fterward, there was this persistent,
full-body humming. Had this vast epiphany been simply
a dream? Was life a dream? Even as I wondered, though, I
knew that the experience had been real. Would these images
come to us all the time if we would just stop and listen and
pay attention to the larger self?

But how could I have been hit by lightning in the
middle of New York City? I had no answers, only a million
questions. This humming—I still feel it today. I feel as
fragile as when I was first born. I am shaking all over. Is
this the "humming" people hear just before death?
Am I dead?

When I did hospice work, people would report hearing
a humming sound in their bodies just before dying. It's a
tremendous noise, like a loud clap going through them.
"The hummingbirds are coming to visit you," I would tell
them. "They're rising in your heart now. Let them enter."

They would look up at me dumbfounded. "Whatever
fears or regrets you have, it's going to be OK," I would say.
"Just forgive yourself now."

Their mouths would be open, and they would be looking at me with wild, glassy eyes. "Whatever you've done, whoever you are, this is your transition. You're being emptied. The Earth embraces you in her grace. Just let go. She is like a cosmic egg, and the egg in your body is vibrating with hers. It's time to go home."

Then I would begin to see the luminous, peach-colored egg in their bodies move out, returning a part of themselves to the Earth. "She was your protector. Her gift to you now is your clearing," I would say. "Everything is all right. This is the sound of your freedom. It's time to leave your body. Leave through the top of your head. Discern the light. Go to it."

I have held dying people in my arms as the humming coursed through both our bodies. In myself, the humming was only slightly audible. Empathically, I would sense the other person's feelings in order to make the passage smoother. In that moment, I could feel them releasing years of accumulated pain, betrayals, lies, anger, memories, and attachments to other people.

With their recognition of the light, they would begin crying or wandering above their heads, coming back into their bodies, looking at me like a child for support. "What's happening to me? I'm not afraid. I just feel so much joy. I'm going to go now." And then they would die.

Before my friend Maria died, she kept repeating the words of the Buddha: "The world is a bridge. Don't build your house on a bridge."

I miss them, but only the living grieve for the dead. The dead are happy in their humming. The hummingbird brings celestial music to people who are dying. A hummingbird dies quickly when confined in a cage. Its only mission is to spread joy. If it cannot do that, it destroys itself.

That's me, I thought. If life becomes a prison, if I lose
the spirit of joy and get caught in other people's dramas and
pain, I'll just die suddenly in a flash. I need the lightning
to stay alive. Life is so fast. I need to go in every direction at
once, wherever the flower of devotion in my heart takes me.

During my years of working with the practice of conscious dying, I have seen birds come at the moment of death
to sit at an open window in the dying person's room and sing
to the passing of the soul. Birds are harbingers of the soul's
flight back to the Creator. Their songs are the call home, the
joy of release into another world. There can be a celebration
of death when the birds come to sing of a new life elsewhere.

In March 1985, I truly lived my dying and died while
living. The humming sound penetrated the core of my being
and purified my body and soul. My personality and ego
finally surrendered totally to something greater than myself.
I felt loved, cherished, warm, in awe, and at home on Earth
for the first time.

In order to be born twice in this lifetime, I do not have
to die physically—I just have to surrender. A hummingbird
conserves its energy at night by slowing down its heart and
going into a deep sleep, like the yogis in India. I do not even
remember breathing after the lightning struck me. To die to
the old self *consciously* is the great thing for which we spend
much of our adult lives preparing.

For weeks after my near-death experience, I felt like I
was gliding above the Earth, like a bird. I felt the paradox of
being both dark and light, on the Earth but not of it. Since
that time, I have learned to live in the "not-knowing," the
paradox, and not to try to find answers to questions. Now I
live in the questions themselves. I articulate them to the best
of my ability and wake up each morning asking for another

question. In this way, I live myself into very intimate, personal answers.

As the days went on, I had to learn how to ground myself. I imagined sending roots to the center of the Earth from the base of my spine. Sometimes I had to imagine steel pipes or metal shafts in order to ground myself. I wanted to walk the "Beauty Way," with gratitude toward all beings— the Nizhoni Way of the Navajo. A "good-medicine" death is when we surrender to the web of life, the Web of Wyrd in Anglo-Saxon sorcery, feeling our interdependency with all living things, and walk out of our bodies consciously. We can prepare for that by walking the Beauty Way while we are still alive.

The only time I can remember a kundalini awakening quite like this—and this was a massive one—was when a bird flew onto my head when I was seven or eight years old. During their migrations, starlings would sometimes blacken the sky over our house in New York and squawk all night in the trees. I would stare at the masses of birds and clap my hands for them to disperse. But one day a black starling landed on me and would not leave. I was walking in the garden with one of my sisters, when this bird shit on my shoulder and stayed on my head for twenty minutes. That was when I first heard the humming and left my body to fly with the bird tribes; in those days, my higher self would appear in the form of a giant bird.

As my sister ran laughing to get her camera, the top of my head blew open and my pineal gland became very active—I suddenly saw with new clarity. I did not know about the pineal gland at that time, but I started to stick my tongue way in back of my throat, an old yogic technique. After that experience, I could understand the lan-

guage of birds. I learned their migration patterns and how
they navigated magnetically by attuning to the Earth's poles
and ley lines. When my sister returned with her camera, the
bird casually flew off.

A few days later, I went walking in the garden of our
family home on Long Island—in the same place where the
bird had sat on my head—and saw a woman dressed in a
black cape with a hood. She had long black hair, curled at
the ends, and piercing brownish-black eyes. This specific
area, I later learned, was the site of great underground water
domes. The domes had given rise to all my multidimensional
experiences.

Meeting this woman was my first meeting with the
Goddess. I fell in love with her immediately. I was so excited
to see her that I ran toward her at full speed and fell right
through her disappearing body. She was transparent, like
a hologram. I dubbed her the "Lady Venus" and vowed
to meet her again, even if she was not solid.

That was when my dreams of Inner Earth began. I never
saw real fairies or elves in my parents' gardens, but I did see
them in my dreams nightly after my pineal gland had been
activated. The elves and fairies told me they were my guides
and that we were of the same blood. These beings were
ancient tribal races that were clairsentient and interbred
with humans and then vanished into another dimension
like the Dreamtime.

George, the king of the elves, was my male guide, and
Gwynhwyrr, whom I had once known as a fairy but who now
lived on the Pleiades, was my female guide. They taught me
to fly by twisting my body into a funnel of wind. Soon I
would be soaring, visiting ships in the skies with apples on
their tables laid out by the sky people. The ships had lots of

elevators and decks to traverse. As a child, I loved to ride in them because they were so fast. I saw parallel realities, an ocean, and farmers who lived in another dimension in the same physical area where my family lived. George and Gwynhwyrr would take me to a hole in the backyard, which I would use to journey to the underworld, to the center of the Earth.

I loved this hole in the backyard because it was so big. I felt it could contain the whole world. I imagined journeying from its bottom through a system of tunnels that ended in an elfin room with a cozy table and chairs, a fire, food, and lots of busy elves. They would instruct me to lie on the hardwood table, and then they would put crystals that lit up inside my body. It never hurt. I remember waking up remembering where the crystals were and how to use them—that this one was for accessing the Earth and this one for the Pleiades and so on.

In 1985, after I was struck by lightning, I began to have the same dreams I'd had when I was a child. As an adult, I had suppressed every memory of elves and fairies and my childhood dreams. This time their message was clear: "Wake up—you are a seer. This is the time of the reincarnation of fairies and elves and the spirit of Atlantis. You have come here to work in the media. Prepare for a renaissance of spiritual, scientific, and creative work. You are here to share and release everything you know from all your lifetimes. You must dance, sing harmonically, learn holography, begin a new form of theater, dance the planets in stone circles, and become a storyteller and maker of films. Whatever you do in this life, rainbows of success will arc over your head. Help people raise their consciousness. You will know what to do.

Do not do *one* thing well; the time for that is over. Do many things *simultaneously* and well." Then I would hear the names Gwynhwyrrr and the Pleiades and wake up.

It took a long time for my rational mind to accept and believe all this; however, in the midst of this process a curious thing happened. My father was selling the house I had grown up in, and I decided to return there. I went back to the hole in the backyard, but it had since been filled in with dirt. Then I felt drawn to the basement, to a hole in the wall.

I didn't remember making this hole to store childhood maps and stories, but there they were: numerous detailed maps of Poseidonis, the Atlantean islands, Lemuria, and Pangaea, along with stories I had written about giants and elves. This was part of the recapturing of my childhood memories. The divine child in me opened my heart as I read each multicolored map, each hidden reference to my future, and I wept.

The moment I returned to New York City, I felt drawn to pick up a copy of *Interview* magazine, something I had never done before. I opened it to an article on a woman named Linda. She was explaining to her interviewer how a large group of human-reincarnated fairies and elves who had last been together in Atlantis were suddenly waking up and having kundalini experiences. She had come from Hawaii to New York to help activate these people, she said, because they would eventually work in the arts and the media. She explained that they had been "timed to go off" and that she wanted to be of assistance to them in their awakening.

Realizing the role synchronicity was playing in my life, I went to see Linda myself. In a tiny, two-room apartment

on Morton Street—a street where I had previously lived—
sat a woman with a deep, throaty voice and "stardust"
makeup above her eyes.

What was I doing here? I wondered. My soul was very
excited, but my personality was waning. As I languished in
confusion, Linda looked straight through me and began to
tell the history of my soul, all the way back to its creation.
She explained how I had loved color and sound and how I had
invented huge organs that, when played, filled an entire
room with color. I began to see all my lives in detail, unroll-
ing like a film. As my awareness heightened, the air in the
room began to crackle. I began to emotionally experience
each life's lesson and each death experience. Each moment
of love and insight swam through my body in a river of
tears and purification.

Linda proceeded to mention Gwynhwyrr by name and
asked whether I would like to talk to her. How did this
stranger know so much? What were the Akashic Records,
and how could anyone read them so clearly? Through Linda,
I talked to both Gwynhwyrr and George, and I cried buckets of tears as I opened the old channel to these two dear
old friends.

That night, I dreamt that a hummingbird entered my
heart and would never leave me until I learned the full meaning of joy and pleasure. Linda had told me, "If you're not
being creative, you're off track." I have always followed her
advice and have never let her down.

THREE

ANGELS

*L*inda was the first person to tell me about the archangel Michael. She said he was an overseer of many worlds and that he would visit me. I thought she was pulling my leg. This was too much: an archangel visiting me in my apartment in New York? I didn't even know if I believed in angels.

After our session, I was lying in bed and felt a presence enter the room. I began to have goose bumps and sat up straight. The room lit up. This was not the eerie green glow people see in out-of-body experiences. I was in my body, wide awake, in a heightened state. Before me were the outlines of three distinct light forms that looked like angels. They began to send me telepathic messages that I had no problem understanding. Large amounts of information were broadcast to my third eye in less than a second. My body tingled. "Look beyond the form," the angels told me. "Blessed are those who do not see but who believe anyway."

The three beings introduced themselves according to the stars or star systems from which they had come: the Pleiades, Sirius, and Arcturus. They told me about love. They told me to cherish my emotions, to help others feel, and to remember the joys of the ways of ancient times.

My body went into samadhi, a deep state of meditation in which there is no duality, only constant bliss. I felt all the channels of my body clearing. I began to see its acupuncture meridians light up, and I witnessed each stage of purification as it was occurring. I have never forgotten that original "blueprint" of the body, and I still use it in my healing work. For a few months afterward, blue-green lights would waft across the room. By then I began to think I was crazy.

At that time, I was working during the day as an artist in the design business. I had started my own company designing clothes and housewares. I couldn't talk to anyone in the industry about what I was experiencing. Lacking a verbal outlet, I began to speak through my work. I scouted a retail space in the Soho area, where I opened a store called, appropriately, Pleiades. There, I designed Celtic suits for men: suits with rune buttons, *vesica piscis* symbols on the collars; violet coats with violet collars inlaid with sphinxes. I constructed silver jackets to hold crystals in tiny pockets over the chakras. I also emblazoned T-shirts with giant ravens, owls, hawks, eagles, and even snakes crawling up the sleeves. Blown up in large letters on the backs were the mystical words "Celt," "Cathar," "Merovingian," "Tuatha DeNaan," "Griot," "Meistersinger," "Eros," "Gnostic," "Avebury," "Bard," and "Serpent Mound, USA."

I also created a "priestess" line of clothing with caduceus collars and rope belts with nine knots. These included Athenian folding gowns with wreaths of dried flowers for the head and bold Native American medicine wheels inlaid on the front or back. I made Navajo blankets into pants, shirts, and coats. I even designed table mats bearing Tibetan seed syllables, Tibetan–prayer-flag shirts, and necklaces of stones gathered from sacred sites around the world.

My business was like a clothing renaissance, ancient in theme but a little before its time. People in the design field thought I was inventive but losing my mind. As for me, I had never felt happier or more balanced in my life. I began to not care what anyone thought of me or what I was doing. Those in the world of glamour, I realized, always looked to others for approval. Many of my friends felt empty in their work and very isolated when they came up with revolutionary ideas.

Since none of my old friends could understand me, I called on Linda for support. I wanted to meet the other reincarnated elves and fairies. She invited me to an evening at a loft near where I lived.

As I ascended the stairway on the appointed evening, I could hear the voices of more than a hundred people. My heart beat faster. I walked in the door, and the hair on my skin shot up. There was a woman—I will call her Rianna—who had grown up in my neighborhood, gone to Georgetown University with me, and yet with whom I had never once had a conversation. Seeing me, she turned around as if to say, "Oh, *there* you are. It's about time you remembered." She came right up to me and said, "I have just woken up. I originally came from the Pleiades. I feel that I know you from there. I am so happy to meet you again."

After holding her for a long moment, I turned around and saw other people I had worked with but never spoken to except in passing. One man I had worked with at the Metropolitan Museum of Art came over and shook my hand. He said, "I am remembering coming from Sirius. This is all happening so fast. I had an incredible experience in March.

I dreamt all night of elves." Thus did I begin to meet my
real family, my spiritual family. The introductions went on
all night.

My father began to think I was having a psychotic
break, and my siblings made jokes about spaceships behind
my back. Everything was timed perfectly. When Shirley
MacLaine's book *Out on a Limb* was published, I sent it to my
parents. Since it came from a respected person of their own
generation, they could relate to her extraordinary experiences
with the Pleiades. As my friends from the past fell away, my
parents began to read books about channeling, alternative
health, and other New Age subjects.

On one of my early-morning walks downtown, I began
to hear the humming again. No, not here, I thought. Then
I breathed deeply and slowed down the sound and heard
an inner chanting: "Om Aim Hrim Klim Chamundayai
Vijaya . . . Re . . . She-Ma . . . Amaru . . . Amapti . . .
Akaee . . . Akaree . . . Amakua . . ." I was calling in the
life force—the higher, middle, and lower selves, and the
ancestors—as in the kahuna and Vedic traditions. No one
else could hear these sounds. I stood startled on the sidewalk,
paralyzed with wonder. I also began to sing what I later
learned were the songs of the *dakinis*—female deities—of
Tibetan Buddhism.

Then I began to dance in mudras: each sound, each chant,
had a corresponding posture. Was I crazy dancing in the
middle of Eighth Street? A man came up to me laughing and
begging for some breakfast money, and I gave him all the
money I had.

For the first time, I really saw the poor. I saw people hun-
gry, begging, frightened, drinking, and lost, and I was filled
with compassion. Something took root in my heart and grew

like the opening of a second sight. These people were not
separate from me. I began to wail in a deep sort of roar, a
gut-wrenching sound from the depths of my belly. I was
overwhelmed by all the hurt, the fragmentation of my soul.

I kept crying out, booming a deep, low tone from my
lowest chakra. I do not want to *survive* anymore, I thought, I
want to *live*. I want to live as if today was the last day. A rose
smell wafted by my nose. I was not alone on this dark street
next to the subway station; I felt the presence of a spiritual
teacher. This was a great heart opening, and I was shivering
with gratitude.

I did not return home for days. I sat on the streets and
lived with the homeless and went to soup kitchens to volun-
teer my help. I opened myself to the world of service. Why
hadn't I become a doctor like my father and helped restore
someone's eyesight? Why hadn't I seen the suffering before?
I held people in my arms, caring for them like they were
members of my own family.

I listened to stories, some so disjointed they were unin-
telligible. Some street people were bloody from having been
beaten. I stayed near anyone who would accept my company.
A few people thought I was an angel, while others thought I
was crazy. Some people had open sores and gangrene that
stank. I brought people food and felt helpless to do more,
except love them. I felt an affinity for these people.

When I finally made it home, I quit my job. Everything
stopped. I took all my clothes, all the most glamorous outfits
that I had worn to numerous nightclubs and dinner parties
and threw them on the bed: Jean Paul Gaultier and Armani
suits, Comme des Garçons jackets, Matsuda coats, the best
handcrafted shoes in the world, Chanel-type coats I had
designed for men. I took everything in my arms—thousands

of dollars' worth of the finest couture—and walked to St. Mark's Square and sold it.

People flocked from all over. Old friends of mine called their friends, telling them I was desperate, selling haute couture on the streets for almost nothing. It was a mob scene. Many of the best clothes—the items people couldn't afford—I just gave away to the homeless. The street people looked very glamorous in them. I had to laugh as their eyes crinkled and lit up.

"Thank you, kind prince, for the royal robes," one drunk man said. A few fashionable people gave me all their savings for a prized jacket. In the frenzy to consume, everyone made up their own prices. I took whatever they offered. In return, I gave each person a gift: a kind word, a short reading of their soul, a crystal, or a stone.

In the midst of all this, I remembered Alice Bailey's book *Glamour: A World Problem*. I no longer cared for glamour. I did not have to possess objects and people or spend my life shopping. Thus, my old life became a past life. It was time to begin all over again. Becoming the holy Fool in the tarot, I had lost everything and found my soul. I still had to face the spiritual glamour of the New Age, but that was a long time coming.

The next thought I had was to build a smaller version of Stonehenge in New York City. I found an empty lot in the East Village and hauled truckloads of blue stones to it. I remembered that Stonehenge was originally blue, and I wanted to accurately reproduce the blue light emanating from the stones under the full moon.

After that, I wildly began to make stone circles all over the city, erecting monuments wherever I felt ley lines crossed. A drunk Native American man began to watch me as I carefully laid out medicine wheels in empty lots. I led him through the four directions, spiraling to the center and invoking the four elements, the four archangels, and "all my relations." He began to help me in my quest to practice urban shamanism.

With the rest of my savings, I paid my rent six months in advance, filled my refrigerator with food, and prayed for a new direction. I fasted, went on urban vision quests, and frequented esoteric bookstores. I read for hours on indigenous peoples, medicine ways, ancient cultures, and the works of Nicola Tesla.

The moment I heard this man's name and read of his inventions and experiments in Colorado, I wanted to recreate what he had accomplished. Soon I was manufacturing Tesla coils in my apartment. Eventually, its floors were crowded with pyramids, copper-wire experiments, turbines, and drawings from Tesla's notebooks. I found a roommate who was a lighting designer. Together we built curved walls and control panels to switch the filters on the Fresnel lights in order to make rainbows arc across the living room.

We bathed ourselves in pure color fields. We studied sacred geometry and created healing environments. We draped the apartment in white cloth and oxidized copper bowls, lamps, and tables into a Pompeiian blue-green color. We set up crystals in corners, placed magnets beneath tables, and painted medicine wheels on the floor.

During this time, Linda called me and asked if I would like to learn about crystals. As I was walking to her seminar, a woman stopped me on the street and handed me a blue quartz crystal, saying, "You have remembered and opened. Here is a gift." Synchronicity was everywhere.

At the seminar, I already knew the names and applications of every gemstone. Linda also showed me a kahuna object. As I held it, I saw a foggy mist. Then, as if on a screen, images appeared of Lemuria, numerous matriarchies, and the various kahuna lineages.

After that, I started to "read" objects in my environment for their hidden stories. I asked for rings, stones, and artifacts. Everything projected pictures, urging me to see holographically as I resonated within its crystalline structure.

Feeling the excitement and drama of life, I wanted to explore and investigate every phenomenon, every mystery: How do other dimensions work? How are images projected here from the Fifth World—the Hopi dimension of nonduality—as synchronicity? I burned with a desire to know.

I decided channeling was the best tool of discovery. Rianna and I often met at the Museum of Natural History in the Gem Room. There, we touched hundreds of large, double-terminated quartz crystals. They became our intimate friends and teachers. The guards would look at us first suspiciously and then in wonder. Putting our hands on the faces of the gems, we would raise our awareness to a feverish pitch. The gems taught us sound healing, easy access to other worlds, and the hidden stories of the Earth.

In these gems, I saw Rianna's fate, her future work in film, her husband and children, and an animated film she would produce on elves. We were both going to realize our future. I recounted to Rianna everything I saw and felt.

When it came time to see my own future, I saw a ruthless tyrant, the facing of my shadow to find the genius, my future work with people's names, and journeying into people's dreams. Then I saw a "green man," a solitary forester living near a community in the woods in solitude, contentment, and peace.

Seeing the probabilities of the future allowed me to connect with an empty place inside me—a place of no thought and no mind, a place of supreme solitude. The inner fire in my womb was glowing now. "You never left the silence," said a voice from within. "You never left the still point."

I realized then that I did not need anyone. The world was a garden, and I had never left it. I was empty, with no boundaries and nowhere to go but *here*. The world never had to change. I relaxed and stopped thinking.

The next morning, I began to channel.

INITIATION

*R*ianna always felt that I could receive
messages from the stars and other dimensions in a simple,
matter-of-fact way. When she came to dinner one night, she
asked if all my elaborate attempts at channeling—putting
tape decks all over the house—had worked. I told her I had
given up, that it was not for me.

As I said it, the room filled with a magnificent presence,
and my throat relaxed, expanded, warmed, and a larger part
of me began to speak. Fully conscious, I began to talk about
creating our own realities and the responsibility we have to
bring together the psychology of the West and the spirituality of the East. It was time to be in our bodies and to love
them, I said—time to be touched. We should cherish our
forms while we are in them, because the other dimensions
are very different and often formless. We should feel while
we still have skin.

That night and later, I talked as though through a radio
receiver. I discerned voices, identifying them as Archangel
Michael, the Star People, the Tree People, or the Inner Earth
People. Eventually, I could talk to my entire consciousness

as a collection of spirits connected to me in the web of life.

Over time, different spirits became allies and taught me how to ask old relatives to leave their grandchildren's bodies. My allies told me what illnesses other people had and how to scan bodies and accurately pinpoint diseases or negative energies. Studying *Gray's Anatomy*, I began to do psychic surgery on people. Talking to the spirits, I began to see the unseen worlds, greeting various grandmothers and grandfathers of the Dreamtime. A whole new world opened up for me.

Rianna and I began shamanic drumming and drummed ourselves through sky journeys and underworld journeys to sacred mountains, brought people's souls back, met teachers, and worked consciously in dreams. With permission, we even entered other people's dreams. In some dreams, I went to wars and helped refugees or assisted the dying victims of major earthquakes. Often Rianna and I would counsel and do bodywork on others in their dreams. The spirits were my friends. I respected them, and they never did any harm to anyone.

Before too long, my phone began to ring. Hundreds of people flooded my apartment for channelings and healings. "Could you ask your guides to tune in for me?" they would ask.

I began to see how each human being was unique and how each person's issues were personal. I also saw that although I could not heal anyone, I could offer advice if it came and channel love while holding thoughts of beauty and perfection. Rianna brought a friend over with a tape deck and started recording the sessions. I accepted gifts in exchange for my work. Though I didn't charge people, I always had enough money.

Clients would ask me such questions as "How did you

know my mother died in a car crash?" or "How did you know I had an abortion last week?" I began to mirror people's souls back to them. If I could show them a clear mirror with all the dimensions reflected in it, they would trust themselves to find their own answers.

I had to gently lead people back to themselves and give them enough information to begin their inner work. I told them the investigation wouldn't be easy but that it would be the greatest work they would ever do. "I don't have the answers," I said, "and I'm not a guru. I'm just like you: a human being becoming fully human."

Soon afterward, I met a woman named Tani, and she became my partner, working side by side with me on clients. After laying her hands on someone, she would offer me her open palms, and I would place the palms of my hands over hers. Then we would start to shake, vibrating with a powerfully directed current.

Tani was remarkable, always exploring and testing her newfound abilities. We would see black holes and whole star systems in people's bodies and say to each other, "Did you see that black hole where she was raped as a child?" or "Look at the star pattern here and the writing on her third eye," or "That person has a triangle on their third eye."

We often let the same channel go through both our bodies, speaking back and forth or talking in other languages we didn't understand but with which we felt a communion. Other aspects of ourselves would have conversations across the table, singing songs to each other and then bursting out laughing. Tani was my sister of the Dreamtime. I knew we had come from a similar place and that wherever we were in the world, I would find her and begin where our last conversation had left off.

Then the sound healing began. I would sit with Tani in a dark room, and we would sing *through* each other. In a state of constant surrender, we would let songs "sing" us and stories "write" us. We learned to breathe deeply from the first chakras in our pelvic areas, storing great, long tones in our lungs. For weeks we practiced "overtone chanting."

Then I went into the silence to sing. Alone for a month, I never spoke words but sang to every form—every plant, every tree, every object. I learned to communicate empathically. I learned the sounds for each color, staying within the field of one color for days. I experienced Creation, the naming of things and the sounds of their essential nature. I experienced pure feeling.

During this time, my phone went unanswered and even everyday interactions took on numinous meaning. I sang my innermost tone, navigating through my body to find the resonance of my heart, lungs, gall bladder, and intestines. I was laying the groundwork for singing in overtones through people's bodies in order to heal their internal organs.

Later on, I worked with cancer cells, singing to them, and began to reverse cancers. I would identify the cancer cells' frequency and then overlay other instructions to the cells in order to help dissolve the disease. To each cell, I would sing the story of that person's soul and how that particular cell was helping in a transformation of matter. Soon, I learned how to fully dissolve some illnesses through sound and intention. I felt the presence of the Nada Brahma, the soundless sound, singing me, and I wanted to share it.

Tani and I began a form of treatment in which we sang through people's bodies, placing them on the floor with patterns of rock and crystal around them in intricate arrays. We

would sing through their cells, moving around their bodies
in synchrony. We would talk to their souls with words as
we identified patterns, cords, and miasmas and lifted them
out of their muscle tissues and cellular membranes. Our
work was powerful. It showed me how two people working together could speed up the natural healing process
exponentially.

One evening, Tani told me it was time for an initiation.
She wanted to lead me through my lion totem. We closed our
eyes and merged our third eyes so that we would see the same
images. We often tested each other to see whether we were
in fact witnessing the same events. This time, we were both
concentrating like lasers.

I began to drift to an altar I had seen in recent dreams. I
had a leonine body and face. Turning around, I saw hundreds
of Lion People lined up in rows and beings from different dimensions with animal faces. The Andromedan beings and the
teachers from the Pleiades had no form, while the Paschats,
the Lion People from Sirius, were quite substantial.

Walking up the altar, I saw a throne and two tall, leonine
beings standing erect waiting to pass me an adz. They put
a robe on my shoulders (like a star quilt) and looked at me
with familiarity and joviality. They explained that they were
projections from the fifth dimension, a means of teaching
through archetypes. They said they were as real as I and
would remain in direct communication with me if I ever
needed them.

They began to sing a song that felt very East Indian. This
was a galactic initiation, much like the Buddhist Kalichakra
is on Earth. The Dalai Lama performs the Kalichakra, in
which people dedicate their lives to the service of all sentient

beings and receive new names linked to Shambhala, the Tibetan spiritual kingdom. My new name, they said, was Solan—Young Eagle.

I explained to the beings that I did not want to be a member of any mystery school or secret teaching but that I wanted all occult or hidden information to be revealed for all to understand. I did not want to be treated like royalty; I wanted to be ordinary, equal to everyone else. All come from the same source, I said. All are essence. Unbeknownst to me, in so saying, I passed my initiation.

In other lives, I had experienced initiations in temples where I was sexually abused, homosexually raped by male priests, or inducted with bizarre rituals into various orders. Through such initiations, I had developed a revulsion to elitism and secret societies that used control and manipulation. As in manhood, marriage, or the opening of the third eye, initiation is a rite of passage of the heart. As I released the emotional and sexual molestation of the past and the darkness of all the magicians I had known, initiation took on the simple meaning of a new beginning.

I had been a monk, a hermit, and an ascetic for too long. Now it was time to be initiated into the world, into the knowledge and experience that, when integrated, eventually becomes wisdom. I needed more than the East Indian teaching of self-realization. I had discovered the silence of the higher self; now it was time to be in the world.

It was time to go to Glastonbury, England, to satisfy a deep longing for Avalon on Earth and to see the zodiac, the "circles of twelve," in the landscape. Rianna had just returned from Glastonbury, where she had climbed the Tor and seen a huge mandala of fire and color in the sky. Tani and I were ready for an adventure.

FIVE

GLASTONBURY

*T*he Tor is a majestic oval hill with seven
rings around it, the home of Tuatha de Naan, an initiate
tribe of fairies in Celtic lore. Surrounded by water in Atlantean times, it was the source of the legends of Avalon. King
Arthur is said to be buried in the old abbey there, which sits
on one of the most potent ley lines in the British Isles.

Tani and I walked to Chalice Hill, the site of a sacred
well. We sang a blessing for the Earth, dipped our hands in
the water, and threw some drops over our shoulders. We
talked to the spirits and the landscape angel, who blessed
our journey. The well had a cover with an image of the
vesica piscis, the sacred marriage of male and female, engraved
in stone. The land was full of nature spirits, devas, and elementals. Million-year-old mollusks could be found in the
soil where the sheep grazed. There were marked fairy and
elf paths, circular groves of trees, rock circles, cairns,
and dolmens.

Within twenty-four hours, Tani and I had found a special
shop in the center of town called Starchild. It had a courtyard

with a fountain next to the entrance. In this courtyard, I spotted a group of ten ethereal women in white gowns baptizing children. No one else saw them, but I watched their movements carefully. I saw them bring in a child's soul from the stars and love that child deeply.

It was no coincidence that the store was named Starchild. Carmen, one of the owners, came up to Tani and felt an instant connection with her. Soon she was giving us gifts and asking if we would like to stay in her house on Chalice Hill. Her husband, the co-owner of the store, communed with devas and angels and made tinctures and herbal remedies whose formulas were transmitted to him by the nature spirits.

This couple's home had an elf path going through it, right where Tani and I slept. The elves would walk through our bodies all night, often taking objects of ours with them. We were up almost all night watching them. When sleep finally came, the elves overwhelmed us with images of talismans, runes, cauldrons, giants, places to go to in Wales, and the birthing rituals of ancient peoples like the Nabateans, the pre-Celtic races, and the fairy folk. The ancient Celts, we were told, were from the East, driven to the western margins of the British Isles over time.

I dreamt of the Nabateans and their ancient initiation rites for many nights. The Nabateans immersed people under water until they stopped breathing and died for four minutes. The initiator would keep his or her hand behind the head of the one being submerged, feeling the life force and monitoring the brain activity. When it was time, the initiator jerked the soul back into the body and induced breathing again.

In those few minutes, initiates would have reviewed their entire life on Earth and seen the influences of other lives on their present existence. In this way, they faced their fear of death and made peace with life.

Training for this ritual required the development of a strong will to live and instructions on the workings of the subtle bodies and soul travel. Once revived, the initiates recounted what they had seen and shared it with others for interpretation. This was their baptism, their second birth into a conscious life.

During my dreams in Glastonbury, I learned how to follow underground water. Then, in the waking state, I practiced taking walks following my intuition, focusing my attention on the serpentine paths of water beneath me. Like a dowser, I found water domes, circular groves, standing stones, meandering pathways of animals, and resting areas for deer. Sitting in these places, I drew the life force up my spine from my root chakra. I heard a humming inside the Earth and a voice saying, "Life is water and stone. Life is water and stone. You are the four rivers leading you home." I would sing to the center of the Earth, then tunnel below the soil and follow these rivers. These were the elf paths. The elves and gnomes are the guardians of the Earth mysteries.

Mnemosyne, the Greek goddess of memory, reminded me that her path, too, was serpentine. I learned that sound travels linearly in air and circularly in water. I often felt submerged in the unconscious underwater, picking up impressions of the waking world. The undines, or female water spirits, taught me to read water circles and locate underground oceans. I saw the races of Mer and the first dolphins to become human. I saw a temple in Atlantis where dolphins were allowed to incarnate as humans. After the temple was destroyed, many of the dolphins could not leave their human bodies and return to the ocean. They felt trapped and betrayed.

Our reptilian brain remembers the Nibiruans, also known as the Reptile People, and the dolphins. Dolphin brains link continents together as they navigate rivers under large landmasses. I also remembered Oannes—the root of Johannes, John the Baptist—the god who came from the water to teach the Sumerians. This was Mnemosyne's way, meandering to find the image and meaning of baptism.

This book is a kind of baptism. We plumb the depths of the unconscious together and bring back a new image of God inside us, waiting to be born twice. We bring back a conscious awareness of where we have been, and this becomes the story of our origin. At the right moment, we will all give an account of our stories, the stories of the Earth meeting the sky. That will be a great day, a great sharing. All our stories are part of a greater collective initiation: the birth of our conscious humanity and our rightful place in the universe.

Tani and I met a shaman in Glastonbury who also had seen the birthing temples of priestesses bringing in star children. This man worked with tree spirits. He carved elaborate wooden acupuncture needles that contained the spirits of the trees from which they had been taken. When we lay on his table and held these needles, a warmth came over us, and hidden layers of feeling rose to the surface. Unworthiness, vanity, and insecurity all asked to be heard and healed.

After each emotion was acknowledged, each would relay to us a memory of an event or action from our past and then give us a lesson. During these sessions, linear thinking departed and holographic awareness gained ascendancy. Kinesthetically, we were enveloped in feelings of safety and pleasure, as though in the midst of a thick forest.

Every full moon, the shaman gathered herbs and made potpourris, tinctures, and other medicinal remedies. The air in his office was filled with lavender, the spirits of the mugwort, the branches of oak and elderberry. Placed in the corner of the room were the horns of a stag, a poem to the Goddess, and a cauldron.

The shaman often took us to the countryside outside Glastonbury, where he had created his own stone circles and where he communed with the spirits of the glen. He would ask us to close our eyes and identify the whereabouts of the closest elf. Intuitively I would say, "Right next to my ear, breathing on me," and he would scream, "Right!" He took us to where the elves lived and gathered—places where the air was thick with them staring back at us.

He also taught us to honor and contact the three auric fields of a tree. Once, we walked clockwise around the base of a tree, and I chose a direction in which to pose a question. Leaning on the thick bark with my back, I asked why I had come to Glastonbury. I heard nothing, but I felt the inside cavity of the tree open and a large spirit come out and envelop me. I rose through the trunk to a higher perspective.

Then I heard the tree spirit whisper, "Be still— Glastonbury is your home. You will come back to commune with the spirits periodically. You still have to face the Tor, the blood sacrifices of kings, the burial grounds in Iona, Scotland. Remember to celebrate the cycles of the Earth again. Hear the wind, the pulse of the land, and never forget."

Thanking the tree, I moved away and heard distant flute playing. It was the god Pan. I felt drawn to the music. I became lulled into a deep sleep in the wood, and in my sleep, I went to meet the green man.

First I saw men in black armor galloping furiously along dark roads on horseback. I saw a virile horned god whose body was of the Earth, rooted in the ground. I remembered Carl Jung's story of hearing Wotan and his men galloping past his home in Bollingen at night. I felt I was witnessing the Wild Hunt, hunting for the part of my soul I had lost in Glastonbury. I was hunting myself, looking for my heart across the darkling worlds.

The horned god looked at me. "No," he said, "you are looking for your masculinity. It is wild, untamed by any man or convention. You are a man of the wood, hoofed like us. You are like Robin of the Wood, finding your place, your instincts. You must show men and women how to put the parts of themselves back together—first the thirteen parts and last the new male, the fourteenth, the return of Arthur."

The horned god was lusty, hairy, fierce for the Goddess— a strong Earth steward—and he gave me permission to be the same. True power lay in the instincts, he said. He wanted me to track animals with him, smell before seeing, become very quiet in the woods, and then leap out. He had a tattoo of a bull on his arm. I had to take the bull by its horns, wrestle it to the ground, and lead it instead of it leading me.

The bull was my powerful nature under the control of my will. It was my animus, and I was the bullkeeper, the Mithraic bullfighter facing the minotaur in the ring. I held the bull by its horns and directed the docile creature. For me, that bull became all bulls—all my instincts, hot and furious, wanting to be manhandled. I witnessed Mithras, the ancient

Persian god of light, slaying the bull with a knife to become one with it and assure victory in war.

In my reverie, I recalled that the famous artist Georgia O'Keeffe had collected and painted bull, steer, and ram horns in the desert of the Southwest. She had said that she wanted to be "individuated and alone on the mesa." I felt the desert horns calling me, too. I heard the words "New Mexico."

The horned god looked at me, pleased. "You need to ride wild horses more," he said, "let your hair grow long like the Merovingians, and steward this wild nature within you, lad." Pan played his flute again, and I returned to my body.

The horned god sent me an image of my father during my childhood. My father had already moved to his forest home before my birth. Tall, triumphant evergreen trees ringed the house around the hedges. He had laced the garden with statues of elves, images of pixies and sprites holding lanterns, and signs declaring his love for the garden in old sayings.

My father made me his gardener. I mowed the lawn, raked the paths, weeded the lawns, and fed the birds that we kept in huge aviaries. We collected Mandarin ducks from China, Lady Amherst pheasants, silver pheasants, peacocks, Japanese chickens, tanagers, quail, fantail doves, finches, and cardinals.

I didn't like school or most competitive sports, so I spent all my time exploring and clearing the forest. It was there that I once met a hunter with a pack of dogs. The dogs ran after me howling, and I ran from that hunter as fast as I could. He was middle-aged and wore boots, woolen trousers, and a gray cap. Was he real, I wondered now, or was he a facet of the horned god? I did not know, but I remembered him again, and this time I would not run away.

As a child, I loved to sit in fields of lily of the valley and walk through the marshes after heavy rains. I planted crops in spirals and picked the juiciest fruits from the orchards. I hunted and set traps for opossums in order to keep them from eating our birds. I had a pet raccoon that I let go when it heard the call of the wild.

I balanced on tree trunks, pretending I was in the Olympics in tree balancing. I imagined lumberjacks coming from all over the world, suspended fifty feet above the ground, balancing on huge trees. They would do acrobatics with no nets below. I also imagined giant Lemurian forests with amusement rides going through the centers of trees like tunnels. I saw huge ferns ten times the size of human beings.

The horned god had brought it all back. Now I felt the moss glistening, ripening below me again. I opened my heart and let Khidr, the green man, Robin of the Wood, inside. I felt the greening of the world. War was obsolete, the horned man was the god in me, and I had to have a relationship with him. From that day on, I let my hair grow down my back and wrapped it in leather. I loved my hairy body, was proud of my erections, and felt loud, not wanting to please anyone.

I heard the Tor beckoning. Rising like a monument over the old town of Glastonbury, it can be seen for miles around, like a call to something ancient and mysterious. I started up the first of its seven rings, the base chakra. I saw red flowers, gnarly roots, dead ancestors, and their blood beneath me, fertilizing the soil.

On the second ring, I saw the sun setting, wild sexual fantasies, my childhood foot fetish, the astral levels, the skin on my body becoming warm, sensual, perspiring. I gave the clay shards in my pocket as a gift to the second ring.

On the third level, I saw images of samurai warriors, soldiers of the Rama empire, and all the betrayals, deaths, and separations of the past. I kept saying, "No, I don't want to die yet!" I witnessed how I had abused my power in other lifetimes, how I had indulged myself and lost my soul in vanity and greed, always wanting and expecting more because I had no love or nurturing.

Dizziness swept over me. I looked down as if from a precipice. I felt like jumping, like throwing myself off the edge and drowning in self-pity. I was at once afraid of falling and of becoming inflated and ascending too high. I didn't know whether I could face what I saw. Almost giving up, breathing erratically, I knew I had to jump over the chasm.

I found the stairs on the other side of the hill and saw pilgrims and children easily walking up to the summit of the Tor. I was beside them struggling for my life. Sensing my fear and discomfort, the air elementals ferociously blew more and more wind in my face. Right next to where I was standing there was no wind at all, but I was barely holding on. My feet started to lift off the ground, and I felt myself being hurled off the side.

I dug my hands into the mud, buried my fingers, searching for roots—anything to hold onto. I pawed at the stairway, gasping, crying . . . and gave up. I had failed in my quest. I could not reach the fourth ring of the heart. I left and descended the stairs. The wind stopped. I went to see the shaman.

"There is a nasty spirit who entered your body on the Tor," he said. "You'd better protect yourself. They jump on people's backs and connect themselves to you, in your solar plexus, like parasites. They are a nasty bunch. The Tor, you see, is a battleground of the light and dark forces, a kind of Armageddon. When people are naive or unconscious, elemental astral spirits can take advantage of them and feed off their psychic energy in order to remain immortal. Be discerning on the Tor, and watch your thoughts as they become amplified. The past is over. Let go of the charge on your emotions."

The shaman went on telling me about the Elohim, the "creator gods," who had planted a central spiral in Glastonbury to generate astral energy. He explained that man had to master the astral, balancing the emotions with the heart and head.

"That's why your body is full of water," he said, "to learn about and master the astral element. One day, the elementals will make a bid for power over the Earth, but the invisible Teachers, the Elohim, will return and be ready for them. You have to understand that though you have already chosen to work for the light, you are also a warrior of the balance of light and dark. The elementals are vampires, like televangelists and others who suck the energy of the masses at revival meetings and rock concerts—wherever people willingly give up their power. Many false gurus and hell-and-brimstone preachers are masters of deception. They think they are serving Christ when they are actually serving the dark lords. They talk about Satan, but they have already sold their souls. They are wolves in sheep's clothing."

I listened to him, not knowing what to believe. He exorcised the elemental from my body, and I became exhausted. "Learn discernment, Foster," he warned. "Not everyone is who you think they are."

After that experience, I started to see elementals on people's backs. I saw healers creating elementals and taking people's power from them astrally, draining them emotionally. I saw naive, born-again Christians not in their bodies, thinking the body was sinful, longing to be with Christ in heaven outside themselves and giving away their power to evangelists and pastors who were guided by strange forces. I met people who had had deceptive visions of powerful elementals posing as masters. Elemental demonic thoughtforms hovered over people like bats. I decided to give them no power. I knew who I was, and that was my best protection. I could remain innocent but not naive.

During our stay with her, Carmen began to have memories of her own. She saw herself as a witch who had been tortured and burned to death by a local priest. She needed to release the memories in her body at the exact place where the events had occurred. I asked her for a map and tuned in to it. My fingers pointed to Tewkesbury Abbey.

As we approached the church, Carmen began to sweat. She was reexperiencing how the priest had suppressed his feelings toward her. He had projected his guilt of attraction onto her, accusing her of bewitching him. Then he had ruthlessly tried to destroy what he could not accept in himself. First he had allowed others to brutally rape Carmen in order to release her "spells"; then he had condemned, tried, and burned her near the abbey.

In that life, Carmen had been a woman who loved cats and who collected herbs to heal the townspeople. She had acted as a local midwife and belonged to a coven of wise old women and a few men from neighboring villages who kept the old ways alive. She had loved the festivals of Beltane and Lammas Day and made cornhusk dolls. She had carved Goddess stones for Bridget, Celtic goddess of poetry and culture; Ceridwen, Celtic goddess of inspiration; Taliesin, the wizard Merlin; and the Celtic horned goddesses of fertility, strength, and warriorship. She had slept with an occasional minstrel, bard, or poet, and once in a while had drunk ale at the inn.

After a church was built nearby, Carmen had become more secretive about her potions. Women still came to her home to become fertile or to help their sick children, but it was increasingly dangerous. The priest had taken a liking to her and was afraid of her will and her body—her "magic." Associating cats with witchcraft, he had said his religion was the only true faith. He had destroyed her sacred groves and in their place built churches and monuments to Christian saints. All this Carmen experienced while we were in the abbey.

Then, from the roof of the abbey, Carmen spotted something far in the distance that fascinated and excited her. She was a wonderful, hearty, impulsive woman. She got in the car, navigating by pure feeling and intuition, and drove us to a series of hills in the middle of nowhere. When we reached them, she bolted from the car and ran.

Later we found her sitting in a small, hidden valley. Stones were piled high where an old house had been. This had been her home in the fifteenth century. Lying amid the ruins were her Goddess stones, untouched by time, scattered in all directions. She wept with joy at finding so many talismans waiting for her to come and love them again.

Carmen held both of us, slipping stones into our pockets, beckoning us to take more and give them away so that the old ways would never die. Then she held one large stone to her breast, like a mother might a child, and blew into a hole inside the rock. The sound of the Earth came out of it— deep, alive, pregnant with vitality.

In this life, Carmen was once again in Glastonbury, a midwife who gathered herbs. She now had her shop and a wise, loving wizard for a husband. She was grateful for all our support and help. On our return to her twentieth-century home, we prepared a ritual feast of food and watched films and sang late into the evening.

On the last day of my magical stay in Glastonbury, I went to Wearyall Hill. It is said that Joseph of Arimathea, a close friend of Christ, had brought the cup of the Last Supper to Glastonbury and buried it on Wearyall Hill. Supposedly, the cup carried the dried blood of Christ, shed for the fertility of the land. Joseph had planted his staff in the ground on top of Wearyall Hill, and a thorn tree had grown. This tree, still atop the hill, blooms every Christmas. The royal family in England cut off part of a branch for their Christmas table each year. I felt peaceful there next to the fully rooted tree of Christ, merging with the old and the new.

I had come to Glastonbury to seek my own soul cup, my own grail, and to rediscover the wonder of living. I wanted to reflect on and gain insight into these many events: first the Chalice Well of the Goddess, the union of opposites, and now the Grail Mound of Wearyall Hill, where the chalice is buried. I could feel the sacred container in my own body.

Incarnating on Earth is like carrying a cross of our own flesh and blood. Our spirits are sacrificed to the material universe, experiencing pain and suffering as a form of bonding to all human beings. By learning difficult lessons on Earth, we learn how to be intimate with all creation.

Joseph had brought the cup to Glastonbury to create a bridge between the old and new ways, by honoring both the Christ and the Goddess. The feminine would incarnate as God, and Glastonbury was a center for that birthing process.

I just had to find Herne, the horned god, and his mate, Hathor Maat, the horned goddess—the earthy, beautiful feminine soul in myself.

As in the Arthurian grail mysteries, the Land and I were becoming one. That is what I heard reverberating in my body. Whom does the Grail serve? The god in us becoming conscious, the bridge between the light and dark, the final healing and resolution of polarity on the Tor. We must all hunt ourselves across the dark worlds.

"In a dark time, the eyes begin to see," wrote Theodore Roethke. The Tibetans had always told me the late twentieth century was a dark time, a time of the loss of the dharma, the teaching. The East Indians talked of the great cycle of Kali Yuga, a time of polarity on Earth, and the loss of the knowledge of the golden and silver ages that had come before. For me, I was waking up, finding the New Jerusalem inside.

I walked to the Tor to make my peace. I climbed to the fourth ring and let my heart open, feeling the cup of Christ. I walked to the fifth ring and heard music, bells, dancing, and celebration. The elves definitely wanted me to be a joyful communicator in this life; I felt my throat open wide. The sixth ring was intense, full of visions. I stopped and breathed, clearing away all the images. I felt a one-pointedness in my third eye. I was determined to live my life fully, compassionately, and let nothing get in the way of my happiness. I would change constantly, if I had to, and grow in maturity and respect for all life.

At the top of the Tor, it was peaceful and serene. Standing in front of me were the ruins of a church dedicated to the archangel Michael. I had to use my sword properly this time, for discernment and not for war and self-criticism. I felt Michael's love surround me. He had been my male guide, the sword of the masculine, the mastery of the mind, the Lancelot of the Christian world. He protected those who reached the peak of the mountain. I could see in any direction from here, go anywhere I chose.

Scattered everywhere were crystals, rocks, bits of cloth buried by pilgrims, offerings of gratitude to the Earth. We had all come from far away to know the magic of the land again. I felt the presences of the ancient Celts walking up to me to hold my hand. They haunted this hill and had haunted me to bring my soul here. I felt Avalon inside, and I vowed to them to create a heaven on Earth without violence or compromise.

I had come to value peace of mind on this summit. I slipped into the Dreamtime. I was held by the Mother, and I felt her in the wind saying, "Now leave what you know in the past. Shed your skin and go to Santa Fe."

SIX

THE SHAMANS
OF SANTA FE

I dreamt that Santa Fe was a communications center in the future, attracting artists to the desert, helping them recover from the art market of the cities. That small town of fifty thousand people would eventually become a metropolis. Thousands of people would relocate there to leave the coastlines because of violence, earthquakes, fires, and rising water tables. Eventually, through its mix of Native American, Hispanic, and Anglo cultures and an influx of creative people, it would become a major healing center. When I closed my eyes, I saw all the ley lines of my unfolding destiny leading to Santa Fe.

On the day Georgia O'Keeffe died, seven of us packed into a car and a van and left New York. I wanted to see her home and the mesas where she had walked and been inspired. I kept having dreams of a black snake lying on her bed and hummingbirds in her garden, all trying to tell me something about visionary art. I learned later that these were prophetic dreams.

Every person in those two vehicles had been touched by

55

either a painting of Georgia O'Keeffe's or a photograph of her. The seven of us included Tani, myself, an actress, a film-maker who had been working in Germany, a female corporate CEO, her ex-boyfriend, and the ex's new girlfriend from Germany, who was supporting him financially. The latter two were bound for a Sufi camp in the hills outside of Santa Fe. The actress was a soap opera star. People would always recognize her, and she would blush when they called her by her soap opera name.

I knew this was going to be a wild trip. Only a few hours into the journey, the van's steering broke down, and the film-maker bought a new van, blue and silver. Everyone was reading *The Right Use of Will*, a book by Ceanne de Ronan, which had been written in Santa Fe. Accordingly, discussions of the denial of will and the emotions, as well as expressing and releasing pent-up feelings, were the keynotes of the journey.

I missed Rianna, but I knew that she, too, would eventually be part of an exodus from the big cities to the Four Corners region. I felt we were all voyaging to the heart of the dove, the heart center on this side of the planet. When the new van was bought, it seemed we had all let go of something from our collective past and were now ready for new "vehicles."

Tani and I had been drawing huge crowds at talks in New York before we left. Five hundred people had come to say good-bye to us in a penthouse on Fifty-seventh Street. Everyone at the party had joined in a chorus and sang in harmonics, lifting us all into a heightened state. I had channeled a message from the Pleiades about rainbow tribes, indigenous people and their right to tribal lands, and a later migra-

tion west as far as the Pacific Islands to form experimental
communities guided by native elders.

Unusual phenomena had filled my early days of channeling. My voice had begun to speak in echoes, changing
dialects, and foreign languages I did not understand. A
friend had begun to levitate objects in front of me. The laws
of time and space were changing, but I had wanted roots,
grounding, authenticity, so I had left for the desert and not
looked back.

During the trip, our emotional processing of denial
became a twenty-four-hour-a-day occurrence: in parking
lots, alongside highways, in hotel lobbies—wherever it came
up. Issues of sexual abuse, incest, physical abuse, the blood
of our ancestors, and abuses of power in past lives rose to the
surface like hurricanes. The men bonded with the men and
the women went off together only to meet us later, angry or
teary eyed.

One evening, in Crystal Springs, Arkansas, the women
and I enacted a memory of a past life. They remembered
being in the Middle East together as part of a harem in which
they had served me sensual meals and catered to my every
whim. We exploded with laughter and strong feelings as we
dramatically replayed this and other lives. We all realized
that life itself is theater and that all of us play many roles.
We were learning how not to identify with any one role so
we could be free. By acting out our lives together, consciously and with no attachment, we were free to create new
roles that suited the moment.

A year earlier, I had wanted to experience being buried
alive inside the Earth, releasing any fears of death or claus-
trophobia. I had friends build a box for me to lie in. Dirt was

poured over the box, and I was buried under the ground for one night. I had been training myself to slow down my breath and not to panic.

Underground was a deep darkness. I felt the void of the unknown, and fears surfaced. I kept imagining bugs and scorpions crawling into the boxlike coffin. I examined each negative thought, breathing slowly, releasing my mind from trauma. One of my friends kept a vigil by the grave, listening for my knock in case I wanted to get out.

Dreams had come that night—dreams of buried pharaohs, divine kings sacrificed for the fertility of the land, people torturing me by burying my body while I was still alive. I had seen images of angry animals, too—images of my own aggression. I kept remembering that these were phantoms my mind was creating. Beyond the mind, there is a state of bliss devoid of these fears and gargoyles. I slept in the cramped space and suddenly awakened crying, "Joseph! Joseph!"

I had been dreaming about a man named Joseph, whom I had associated with a biblical story. Out of jealousy, Joseph was sold by his brothers into slavery. Later, in prison, he began to dream and to interpret others' dreams. When the pharaoh heard this, he called for Joseph. After Joseph deciphered the meaning of the pharaoh's dreams, he was freed from prison. Later on, his brothers came to Egypt, and Joseph forgave them and returned to see his father.

On our trip, I remembered this dream. I felt it was telling me to heal my masculine side, to feel my broken heart and open to its gifts. If Joseph had not been sold into slavery and betrayed, his gifts might never have surfaced. I had been through great pain in my life as preparation for becoming a healer. After that experience, I longed to reconnect with my father.

Exhausted from constant processing, our band of seven finally stopped in a campground in Texas. We set up camp on a very exposed cliff overlooking a lake. Afterward, everyone wanted to leave camp and go for a swim. My intuition said, "No. I am not going. I feel danger." Everyone ignored me, saying that if I wanted to create that, it would probably happen.

I had often felt the future, accurately seeing events two or three days in advance. Visions and intuitions in excess of three days were usually more of a probability. All I could predict were cycles: three cycles could mean three days, three months, or three years from now, depending on how my consciousness shifted. I sensed that, in the presence of this group, my shadow had become activated and was now "stalking" me to give my soul a teaching.

I was right. After everyone else had left to go swimming, eight black men in a white convertible drove into our camp. Intuitively, I positioned myself standing on top of the blue-and-silver van and stared as the men approached. They got out of their car and stared back at me in silence, lowering their heads. I read their thoughts and connected myself to the Earth, holding my ground.

The men looked through our bags, opened our tents, and touched the stone circles and crystals we had laid out in front of the site. Then they looked up at me, tall and erect, taking a silent stand. They felt bewildered, looking into my unmoving eyes. I had learned in dreams to look my assailants in the eye and neither to fight nor surrender but simply to hold my ground.

The eight men had been drinking, observing us from a distance. They found only me, awaiting them stoically. They stared into my eyes for a long time, then walked back to their car and drove quietly away.

That was my first test of the shadow. The shadow is not always negative; sometimes it can be a source of great untapped potential—even genius. In this case, however, the shadow was the disassociated masculine, the sociopath who in his aimless rebellion is willing to violate anything. Another test of it awaited us all.

By the time we reached New Mexico, we were tired of camping and took rooms at the Sheraton Hotel in Albuquerque. It was my birthday, July 11, and we had been driving a long time. We all ate dinner out except for the CEO.

During World War II, this woman's father had been a scientist at Los Alamos National Laboratory, helping to create the first atomic bomb. As an adult, she had had a major car accident and had left her body. During her near-death experience, she had met tall beings from Sirius who had told her it was not yet time to die. She had returned to her body, and the beings from Sirius had comforted her. That had been the beginning of her spiritual awakening.

On this particular night, though, she did not want to be part of our group. She isolated herself, feeling intense pain and anger about the patriarchy and authoritarianism in general. This was the same energy that had attracted the men to our camp in Texas.

At dinner, in honor of my birthday, Tani went into trance and read aloud the records of my soul. She read the Akashic Records as we laughed and drank. I felt uneasy, like something was about to happen, but I ignored it.

Meanwhile, our CEO friend was wandering alone

through the streets of Albuquerque's Old Town. Suddenly, a
man came from behind her and tried to rape her, beating her
in the face until she was black and blue. She fought him off
fiercely, digging her rings into his face. At midnight, she
called us from the hospital, her face swollen from crying and
the beating she had taken.

Our friend wanted to go to Santa Fe to recover. She wanted to visit her aunt and an old boyfriend named Damien,
who now called himself a shaman. We were all emotionally
shaken, wanting to take care of her, so we agreed.

When we arrived at Damien's house off Canyon Road, we
informed him of our friend's condition. He and his partner, a
woman named Leah who also called herself a shaman, greeted
us politely. They took our friend into their home and told us
to stay outside.

Soon, we heard piercing screams coming from the windows. Our friend, furious at men, was reexperiencing the
trauma of the previous night. Later, the shamans came outside and told us they had been awaiting our arrival for many
days. It was "time to heal the wounded masculine in all of us,
the ruthless tyrants inside," they said.

I never completely trusted these so-called shamans. I
found their behavior secretive and assuming. On the other
hand, what better way to confront the shadow? Here, I rea-
soned, was an opportunity to face my fears both of shamanism and of power.

I agreed to participate in a seven-day retreat with
Damien and Leah as my teachers, which eventually turned
into six months of shamanic training. The retreat was
attended by a total of seven individuals, including myself
and four others from the original group. It involved seven
days of Vipassana meditation with two meals a day, plus

verbal instruction and bodywork on the last three days.

During the retreat, we all sat and meditated, identifying our thoughts by repeating silently, "Thinking . . .
thinking . . . thinking." Emotions were acknowledged
by repeating, "Feeling . . . feeling . . . feeling." And
noises were identified as "Sound . . . sound . . . sound."
Posted schedules indicated different times for sitting meditations, walking meditations, and meals. The walking
meditations were very, very slow; the intent was to feel
every movement and every muscle. It sometimes took an
hour to walk four paces!

Throughout the seven days, we were constantly told
to conserve water. We took timed, three-minute baths and
didn't keep the water running when we brushed our teeth.
This was called "mindfulness," and we were monitored
constantly. As we meditated, Damien and Leah would read
passages from such books as *A Course in Miracles* (published
by the Foundation for Inner Peace) or Paramahansa Yoga-
nanda's *Autobiography of a Yogi*. Some of the most beautiful
sonnets, journal quotes, and song fragments blended in with
the silence.

By the fifth day, my body felt completely purified of
the negative effects of our cross-country trip. My muscles
relaxed, and I felt my spine ringing and humming again
with kundalini energy. I started to feel ecstasy in my cells.
Food never tasted so good. On the sixth day, we fed each
other with spoons, trying to hold in our laughter, stuffing
each other's faces and spilling our food. We had been told not
to speak or even glance into anyone's eyes for five days, and
we needed a release.

Intermittently, the shamans called us one by one to their
room, where they asked us to pace in front of them. They

sized us up in silence, saying things like, "You are a panther; you walk like a panther stalking your prey." They commented on our progress and asked if we had any needs.

The shamans had created their own form of deep-tissue bodywork that made me yell in pain at the top of my lungs, but they told me to "breathe through the pain" to the other side of it. As I surrendered to their hands during one session, I felt the pain in my abdomen and legs shoot out, and a wave of euphoria enveloped the tender areas.

Damien and Leah also gave talks on how to move our "assemblage points," or "vision spots," the focal points of our spiritual bodies. They whacked us at the base of our spines and pressed on these points to activate new fibers of awareness in our bodies. They told us the assemblage point existed midway in the body and could access any dimension. They said we had to live and breathe and focus all our attention on the assemblage point.

My assemblage point was between my testicles and my anus. Every person's was in a different location. Mine was at the same spot as Damien's. I felt a strong affinity for him that seemed paradoxically to be both an attraction and a repulsion.

After spending so much time in my head and my third eye, I had difficulty breathing deeply. It took all my strength to stay in my assemblage point. The shamans often pulled me aside and said, "You are not in your assemblage point now. Feel the difference. Go back in." I had to learn to rest my weight on the sacrum and let my shoulders fall. I imagined an opening between my legs from which a great light emanated. Closing my eyes, I learned to navigate the room from my assemblage point, seeing kinesthetically through the pores of my skin.

The shamans used diagrams of the chakras and explained their interrelationships repeatedly in brief talks. Finally, to culminate the seven-day retreat, they took us on a meditation through the Solar System. On the night of our journey, other people came to participate, and we were told to remain silent and grounded in our assemblage points without looking up.

The lights went off, and Damien initiated a journey through our local star system with the help of some meditative music by Kitaro. In anticipation of the trip, though, my assemblage point jerked out of position and the whole room started to spin. I wanted to throw up, but I stayed with the music and the shaman's voice.

Now my assemblage point, the focus of all my energies to stay balanced between worlds, shifted to my heart. I heard ringing sounds. Colors exploded. Fibers came out of my solar plexus. I wanted to connect these fibers to the planets. I imagined them moving toward the Sun, to Jupiter, to the center of the Earth. Then I lost consciousness. I felt myself as a ball of light with no grounding, hurtling through the galaxy.

Sweat poured from me as I went through a spontaneous rebirthing. The crowd ignored my contortions, enraptured by their own journeys. I saw that the soul was an egg and that my body was contained inside the soul. Moving the fibers around, I could begin to resonate with birds, plants, and other beings, sending my fibers out to almost any entity simply by willing it.

I left my body and the room and began tingling like a cocoon of light. As a light being, my form could not be seen, but I could see everything: people walking on Canyon Road at night, threads emanating from Sun and Moon mountains a few miles away, and plants with strange glows around them. Shooting fibers from my body, I bonded with plants, rabbits, a stream, and Sun Mountain. I sent out an intention to commune with all different forms of life. Then I returned to my body, exhausted and thrilled. I wanted to keep merging with everything, building stronger and stronger fibers in the process.

That night, my body shone with a radiance, and I dreamed of shapeshifting into a jaguar. My jaguar eyes lit up the darkness in a world of fibers, eggs, and luminous spheres. I experienced my jaguar nature: lean, black, roaming. I felt the union of spirit and instinct. I felt what my body could become. I wanted to learn how to shapeshift *physically* into other animals.

The next morning, in silence, we all went to a Japanese health spa called Ten Thousand Waves, where we had massages and sat in a hot tub. We all felt connected, resting our bodies after a week of intense change. All our clothes had been washed, and our crystals and sacred objects had all been cleansed in salt water. We felt renewed. I signed up for a month more, along with six others, four from the previous group. The next cycle would take place in the mountains, living at eleven thousand feet in the bowl of a glacier.

To prepare us, Damien and Leah took the seven of us to Abiquiu Lake. There, we built a fire and ritually threw all our old clothes as well as our emotional attachments into the flames. We placed all our gemstones on an altar on the precipice of a narrow cliff. One by one, we inched our way toward the altar, offering our most beloved objects and expensive possessions. When we returned, thousands of dollars' worth of gems and jewelry were gone—pushed off the edge of the cliff.

After that, I began to have suspicions about the shamans. What would drive a person to do such a thing? I wondered. I asked myself if I was naive, and I resolved to remain alert. From then on, I watched them like a hawk.

The next day, we stopped in Española to collect stones for a sweatlodge. After we had hiked a long way into the hills to find the stones, Damien and Leah instructed us to form two lines, one for women and one for men. Then they told us to throw the stones to each other like an assembly line. By the end of the exercise, the line of men had collected many more stones than the women.

Then the shamans said to try again. This time, though, they sent strong positive energy to the women and negative thoughts to the men. The men dropped stones, exposing all their weak links and becoming suddenly tired. They also sent negative energy to certain people without telling them. They never betrayed their thoughts or intentions with so much as a look or gesture.

We watched different individuals suddenly lose their concentration. The shamans were teaching us the power of the mind to direct thought. Eventually, we transported fifty stones three miles with this method, all the way back to the car. It was raining the whole time. They kept projecting thoughts that it was easy, and it was.

Then they blindfolded us and led us into the van. They drove us to Apache Canyon, where thirty-foot-high cliffs overlook a stream. There, we were lined up, blindfolded, and all asked to hold onto a thin rope and hike the cliffs together.

We stumbled and knocked into each other. Damien and Leah told us to see through our bodies, our fibers, to reach out from our assemblage points to the landscape. "See through your feet," they said. "Feel the path beneath you."

Just as I was getting the hang of it, my feet slipped and my body began to fall off the edge of a narrow cliff. For no apparent reason, I began to laugh loudly. I could not see what was happening. I felt a hand grab my wrist and pull me up. Had I not let go of the rope in time, I would have pulled everyone into the chasm below. I knew it was Damien who had saved my life. I trusted him more then, at least physically.

When we reached the top of a waterfall, the shamans told us to take off our blindfolds and all our clothes for an experiment. When we walked into ice-cold water and began to shiver, they told us to think, "Heat, warm sun, tropical beach." We all concentrated, and the water began to feel warmer. In fact, soon we were all boiling hot. Then they said, "Think cold, freezing ice, arctic storms, blizzards." Losing circulation, I suddenly jumped out of the water. When we began to think heat again as a group, my body fully relaxed. I felt I had mastered the rudimentary lessons of mind over matter.

My father was a hypnotist as well as a neuropsychiatrist when I was growing up. He had made tapes on hypnosis for my sister's high school psychology class. I had been the most susceptible to hypnosis in my family, able to reach deep trance states; therefore, I had been the guinea pig for a series of guided tapes. Deep in my mind, I knew I had done this in Atlantis with my father and that he had been taught how to control the mind through subliminal messages. Programs and hidden messages had been beamed into work areas in Atlantis in order to control the population.

I was just nine years old when my father introduced me to biofeedback and hypnosis. I would slip into his office, put the headphones on, and turn on the tapes to relax the nerves above my eyes or to control the temperature in my hands. I became very accomplished at raising and lowering the temperature of my hands. I would listen in the headphones for a sound slowing down if I was doing the exercise correctly. I learned to control the sound, making it slower and slower, mastering its rhythm and my own pulse.

My father and I had charted our biorhythms. He had felt that I was learning to become a *sadhu*, or Indian yogi. Perhaps my father had been my teacher in India in another life. At any rate, he was Anglo-Indian in this life, born in New Delhi and raised in Lucknow. He was the first person to teach me mind-over-matter techniques, and they always came easily after that.

The last preparation by the shamans was a gentle surprise: a trip to Georgia O'Keeffe's former home in Abiquiu. They drove me blindfolded up to the door, not informing me where I was. I walked up to the window and saw a black snake and knew from my dreams where I was. I had traveled here before.

Leah took me to the garden in front of the house, next to a statue of Saint Francis. A hummingbird came and rested on her shoulder, and she said in amazement, "Saint Germaine is here." She said we needed to concentrate on why I had been brought here. I told her my dreams and explained how I felt Georgia O'Keeffe was a visionary artist who loved color and that many people would come to New Mexico in search of spiritual and sexual freedom and new forms of art and creative action.

We both sat down and closed our eyes, and the first image I saw was a wheelbarrow. I blurted out, "We must put the broken wheel back together. There is one broken wheel."

Leah jumped to her feet and began digging. She dug all

over the garden and found parts of one wheel. Then she took my hand and led me to a side of the house I had not seen. There, standing upright, was an old wheelbarrow that seemed to be missing a wheel.

A circle was being formed then between the shamans, my friends, and myself. In six months, I would be the one to break the wheel and find the missing parts of myself on my own.

SEVEN

THE RUTHLESS TYRANT

*T*he shamans let go of their rented house on
Canyon Road and left us to pack it up. By now, three of the
people in our original group had left: the woman who had
been beaten, her ex-boyfriend, and his German girlfriend.
Tani, the actress, and the filmmaker were still left. Altogether there were six apprentices. The two new arrivals were
a man named Bob, who was a gentle leader, and a young
woman named Eliza, who had studied kundalini yoga. They
both lived in Santa Fe.

Bob had lived at the Lama Foundation, north of Taos,
New Mexico, for many years and was a hermit by nature. His
motivation for joining our troupe was to be on the edge of
transformational work. As we packed up the house, we began
to feel an intimacy, as though we were making friends for
life. All of us expressed doubts about the shamans, but we
were beginning to feel like a tribe. Damien and Leah kept
telling us they had had a specific vision of seven future leaders coming to study with them. We had arrived on their
doorstep to be initiated. The curriculum would have to be

created as we went along, they said, but anything was possible.

Damien had previously been a marine commando who trained soldiers in arctic conditions. Born in Scotland, he had also been a diver on oil rigs, a marathon trainer in New York, and a fitness instructor who combined yoga and aerobics. He was a soldier to the core, with a pronounced mean side. On the day we cleaned up the house to leave, he gave Leah a black eye.

Leah was from one of the families that came to America on the Mayflower and had moved to Santa Fe from Mill Valley, California. She had been an executive in a record company while beginning her shamanic work. She often communicated with the spirit of a young girl named Jenny, who had died of cancer. Jenny was always around her, speaking to her from the other side.

Something was definitely off here, I thought: Damien had given Leah a black eye, and Leah was talking to a dead girl. What was I doing with these so-called shamans? Couldn't *anyone* call themselves a shaman nowadays? Was my hook to stay with them some sort of spiritual expectation, or were these two simply recreating the patterns of my dysfunctional family?

What I didn't know then was that Damien and Leah were recreating the archetypes of the ruthless tyrants. She was the Madwoman, and he was a combination of Judge, Rebel, and Killer. Later, partly as a result of my work with them, I would be prepared to work with the mentally ill, entering their minds and returning their souls to their bodies. This was the beginning of a hair-raising journey.

On the way to our glacier base camp, Damien made us hike with the equivalent of our own weight on our backs.

This was excruciatingly difficult on steep mountain inclines or while jumping across chasms. We had packed everything we would need for a month in the wilderness with little or no outside contact.

We hiked eleven miles in from the Santa Fe Ski Basin, past Nambe Lake to a glacier bowl filled with large boulders. We had to set up camp and carry more than our weight in water from the streams below. The hike was almost straight down. The water was heavy and jostled back and forth. We were being tested, and my masculine side would learn to take action and endure.

Our menu included rice, beans, almond butter, bread, a few vegetables, wild herbs, bark, and roots. We had millet, raisins, and almonds for breakfast. The work establishing our permanent camp was relentless. We built shelves out of twigs, a large fire pit with a grill to cook on, and a dining table made of large stones with moss laid in the gaps. We planted flowers in the moss that bloomed until we left. The situation was a complete return to the wild. It seemed to be turning into a heaven on Earth.

Damien set up an obstacle course straight out of military school. We had a chin-up bar on the trees, spears to throw, wide gaps to jump across, stations for pull-ups, push-ups, running in place, and everything else a marine commando might want. We had to do the whole course every morning, sometimes twice if we gave up, and our performances were timed with a stopwatch. Breakfast came only after successful completion of the course.

I had never been in the military, but I found that I wanted to test myself for strength, endurance, and agility. I wanted to prove to everyone in the group that I was a strong man who would not break under pressure or fatigue. The first time I completed the course, I was thrilled. The approval was intoxicating.

I had hated gym classes as a child because I had once seen a gym instructor beat up a sixth grader and scream at him until his body shook. I hated that teacher and had never wanted to go to his class. Damien was that teacher incarnate. He yelled, called you sissy, or jumped up and down in excitement if you broke a record, like thirty push-ups in the time allotted. Everyone cheered you on as you went through the ten stations. We all wanted to perform perfectly in order to receive the shamans' approval.

We also had to fall from trees and rocks in what were called "trust falls." Sometimes Damien would have us fall ten to twenty feet backward off a precipice into the arms of the group. If we landed too hard or roughly, we had to repeat the fall. We also rappelled off cliffs and did strenuous rock climbing.

Damien had us men hike twenty-six miles a day until our feet were full of calluses. He pushed us to the limit and then said, "Break through the pain. Give it to nature. Go through the pain and send it to your assemblage point and then out your feet through the inside muscles of your legs. Do not give up."

Damien kept telling me not to slouch under the weight of my pack. He made me imagine white cords from my solar plexus to our future destination, drawing on the energy of the place we were going to. "Rest your pack on your sacrum," he said. "Go into your assemblage point. Draw on the energy of the Earth. Listen to the grandmothers."

With medusa hair, a beard, and dirt all over my clothes, I started to feel like a wild banshee. When no one was looking, I even ate the bark and roots of trees.

Leah woke us up every morning at four o'clock, when the world was still. We meditated as a group, then listened to the wind, the spirits, and different masters, the teachers of the Dreamtime. We wrote down our impressions and shared them with the group. Leah devised many exercises to strengthen our intuition. She helped us listen. When we felt blocked, she came up behind us and sent tremendous waves of energy up our spines. She reminded us that women have great power. Women were the Dreamers of the Flower Worlds, she said.

Our campsite consisted of two main tents or lodges. One tent was a huge dome for meditation, teachings, and ceremony, with an altar we all took turns meticulously cleaning. The second was called the Dream Lodge, where we slept either with our heads together or side by side for warmth. We set up a dozen smaller tents for food, clothing, and cooking. The landscape was alpine wilderness: huge, erect boulders in a glacier bowl carved like an amphitheater out of the rock face. It was stark and penetrating, like our work.

During the first week, we were instructed to find areas for our vision quests. For three days and nights, we would have only water to drink or nothing at all if we wished. We were assured that visions would come. A tent and a journal would be allowed on this particular type of quest.

We gathered wood for a sweatlodge to purify us for our quests. I was chosen to build the pit and the sacred mound in front of the lodge door. There, all our sacred objects would be placed during the ceremony, along with our dreams of purification. It poured rain the day we went to collect willow for the structure. We were knee-deep in runoff and surrounded by deer. We laughed, falling in the water, but the deer didn't run away. I felt the presence of the horned god then. He was telling me to stay and go through the whole process. This was for my psyche and the opening of the Fifth World of the Maya, the World of Flowers.

The day of the sweat was filled with magic. The deer walked right up to me that morning, and I was pleased that we didn't have to do the obstacle course. Gnarly branches I had never seen before lit up on my morning path. Butterflies lit in the women's hair. The forest elementals seemed to love the fiery wood and stone. Etheric salamanders danced wildly in the embers, revealing their swirling, twisted shapes. Elves tripped me in the forest, and I loved their game, cajoling them to do it again and again.

The feast was prepared beforehand, from our most precious supplies of food. We carved a hard wooden shovel to bring the stones into the sweat. All of the preparation was done in pure love and with great, forceful intent.

We took off our clothes in silence, praying to Great Spirit and Grandmother Earth, blessing each stone again and again and honoring the Four Directions. We laid our sacred objects and medicine bundles on the mound and entered the sweatlodge. I had collected herbs for the ceiling, and we all could smell burning sage, cedar, and sweetgrass in the air.

As we did each round, one for each direction of the Medicine Wheel, new songs came. The women sang in high voices, and the men sang in deeper tones. Each of us purged our souls, admitting our deepest fears, blocks, and madnesses. We transmuted our pasts in the burning of our flesh and the falling of our perspiration onto the soil. I saw lights flickering on the ceiling of the sweatlodge and wondered if anyone else saw them. Throughout most of the sweat, all our eyes were closed, deep in prayer and preparation for the vision quest the next day. The lights faded, and I felt the beauty of the dark.

That night, Tani left the Dream Lodge, running excitedly toward the moon. She wanted to leave her body, leave the Earth, and run from her fears. Damien left the tent to find her. We heard her screaming and crying. Damien returned to the tent hours later with rips on his skin and scratches on his legs, all acquired while fighting the wrathful deities who were trying to possess Tani's body.

Tani did not love her physical form and tried to leave it every chance she got. She had had great difficulty jumping over the poles in the obstacle course and was beating herself up for it. She was trying to be a warrior but felt she was failing. She felt ashamed, unworthy of our company. She wanted desperately to believe that Leah was the medicine woman she had tried to find in New York. She was nervous and frightened, and all her beliefs of being an unloved child had risen to the surface.

Damien became frustrated with Tani's attempts to leave and gave her ultimatums: "If you do not stay in your body, we will take you back to town and leave you there. Make a decision now." That authoritarian voice would get stronger the minute we left the wilderness.

My vision quest was a time of solitude and rest, a gathering of inner power and a reconnection to all creation. I dreamed of Thunderbeings and rain dances. The Rain People are the purifiers of society, bridging the gap between nations. They bond to spirits and human beings alike and call in the wonder of the rain. I saw dances that I later tried to duplicate. The Thunderbeings told me I would meet people in the future with whom I had danced before and that together we would remember the rain dances and the Deer Dance.

I learned a great deal about rain on my vision quest. Lightning signals the rain, which quenches our spiritual thirst. The hummingbird's wings are the rain drums that would call in the Great Purification between the years 1992 and 2012. This was the end of a twenty-six-thousand-year Great Mayan Cycle and the beginning of renewal for the Earth. During my vision quest, I was told to bring the rain and to talk to the Thunderbeings. It rained the entire quest.

Animals walked fearlessly up to my tent. My heart leaped when squirrels, chipmunks, birds, beavers, deer, and marmots ventured so close I could touch them.

The second night, I dreamed of a photon belt, a cloud of solar radiation that was influencing the Earth. This belt, my dream told me, had first enveloped the Earth in 1962 and would return again in the summer of 1992. This phenomenon came through the Pleiades and would bring great light and heat to the atmosphere. The Seven Sisters of the Pleiades told me that this photon belt would be perceived by many as a great humming across the Earth. They said Taos and many sacred centers on the planet would vibrate with its arrival. They explained how 1962 was only a preparation and that 1992 was the real beginning of the Earth changes— accompanied by an exponential increase in the amount of pure light transmitted from the Pleiadian star Alcyone.

The third night, I dreamed of solar sheep. These sheep were aggressive, impulsive, temperamental, and adventurous. They represented the Ram archetype, or unreflected masculinity, a masculinity that could not wait for a response from the female side. I felt that Damien and I shared this Ram nature and that we would resolve it together.

Then I saw a giant serpent waiting to devour me. It was

rainbow colored and waiting in the center of a spiral. I had come on the vision quest to shed my ego, to heal the Ram and be cleansed by the rain, and to see the vision of the light coming from a sun in the Pleiades.

After our vision quests, we were once again awakened at four o'clock in the morning to communicate with the other dimensions. It was then that I had a vision of a different map of the stars. In my vision, I saw the word *archaeastronomy* and began to write mathematical equations using Pythagorean symbols. I kept saying, "$E = mc^4$." I explained to the others that Earth was very close to the Pleiades and the Sirius system and that Earth actually rotated around Alcyone.

At 4 a.m., or "yogic time," as we called it, insights and flashes came easily. Buddhists use this time of the day to meditate deeply in the silence. I always channeled at this time, listening to find out about the herbal properties of plants, messages from the Pleiades, or ways to serve our group. I saw that at Harmonic Convergence in August 1987, sacred sites all over the world would break their seals of veiled knowledge. Often I channeled at the shamans' request, learning about their intimate lives and developing compassion for them.

In the wilds, the men and women in our group began to differentiate. The men played drums at night, while the women danced. We also created different medicine wheels and ceremonies. The men's medicine wheel consisted of the Wise Man in the north; the Artist, Sculptor, and Builder in the east; the Father, Latin Lover, and Nurturing Man in the south; and the Rebel, Adventurer, and Wild Man in the west. In the center of the wheel were Eagle and Jaguar, the masters of the wheel who could go in any direction.

The men often painted their faces and stood at different

directions to draw in the Spirit Keepers. The women discovered their wild sides as well as their femininity. They connected to the Goddess in her many forms, as well as to a deep feeling of empowered solitude and self-containment. The women were great dreamers and loved the World of Flowers, learning to face the dark side and the serpent in their dreams.

A woman was put in the Rainbow Lodge during her menstruation to celebrate her blood and commune with the Mother by herself. A woman was esteemed during the time of her "wise wound" and learned to access her strength then. The men chopped wood, carved walking sticks with knives with which Damien had gifted us, and carried buckets of heavy water. My walking stick had Nordic runes carved in it, as well as pawprints and human handprints for protection.

Each of us carved three sticks. One was the perfect walking stick, while the other two were used as javelins. The men threw spears, wrestled, and yelled like hunters. The women created pieces of Goddess jewelry and conducted secret ceremonies for facing the demons in their dreams who threatened their intuitions.

The men also planted crystals at the junctures of ley lines on seven peaks in the Sangre de Cristo Mountains. Each crystal was buried with an intention to honor the Earth and to love her back to health. We also prayed for the healing and purification of humankind. We bonded through these acts.

We even had a ceremony in which we doused each other with whiskey. A peyote and ecstasy ceremony further sealed our unity in the Dreamtime. But I yearned for something less ecstatic and more real, and I received it. I felt that I was truly in my body and fully alive, especially when I went off into the wilderness to track animals or sit on a mountaintop.

Toward the end of our stay in the wilderness, we started a

theater in the mountains with candles glowing on rock cliffs. We acted out archetypes and lampooned the shamans and each other. I loved our teasing, keeping each person in his or her place with humility.

One night, I told an old Gnostic tale called "The Hymn of the Pearl." It goes like this:

> There once was a prince from a far-off land who was promised he would become king if he completed a special task. He had to travel to a place far from home and face a dark beast who guarded a pearl of great price at the bottom of the ocean. If he defeated the beast and found the pearl, bringing it safely back, he would be crowned king.
>
> The prince set off on his journey, taking forty days and forty nights to arrive at his destination. Tired after his long undertaking, he went to a pub in the port town. He drank some ale, and the local fishermen began to talk to him. They offered him work and a place to stay.
>
> He took them up on the offer. He dressed like the townspeople, ate their food, and fancied a beautiful local woman. Before long, he became indistinguishable from the fishermen and completely forgot about his quest for the pearl.
>
> Meanwhile, the prince's parents became worried, since much time had passed without word from their son. They decided to send their son a dove with a message reminding him of his true purpose.
>
> The dove flew to the tavern where the prince was drinking with his mate. Only the prince could see the dove, even though it flew into the tavern through an open window and rested on his shoulder. The dove's message went into the prince's heart, and he began to remember his mission and who he was.
>
> Immediately, the prince walked out of the tavern and dove into the ocean. Deeper and deeper he dove until he

came upon a beast. The beast was the embodiment of all his fears, complexes, and negative thoughts. He became frightened at first, but then he realized that the beast was not real but only a mirror of his own mind. He had to face himself. He must try to understand the nature of the beast in his own psyche.

Sensing the prince had no fear, the beast moved aside. The prince then dove to the bottom of the ocean, where he found a huge oyster. He opened the oyster and retrieved the largest pearl he had ever seen. That pearl was his soul. With it, he returned safely to his kingdom and became a wise and compassionate king.

Our theater on the mountain was filled with such stories, myths, and dramas. During these presentations, we all became at different times the embodiments of wise old men and women, gorgons, rebels, madmen, dragons, princesses, and more. We also made masks of our higher selves, our shadows, our "star lives," and any attributes we wanted either to release or to integrate more fully.

The whole process of making the mask was shrouded in mystery. Each of us would have someone else mold the mask onto our face, and we would have to perceive what we were becoming. We would then decorate our mask, absorbing the other person's vision of us. When it was time to "dance" the mask in front of the group, we had to choose the dance music while blindfolded. We would often sit stunned to discover how perfectly the music fit the mood of the mask.

Hidden selves would emerge during the dances. Anger and rage were ritually contained and released through the persona of the mask. I once became a jester, lampooning the seriousness of the process. Another mask I made was silver, with the words "I Am" written on the forehead. On Halloween, my mask and costume were wild, black, and lascivious, bristling with thorns, branches, and cobwebs.

For those of us who were students, all this was a high form of play. We never identified with one role but created dozens of faces, personas, and outfits. We learned not to take life so seriously and to love each illusion without claiming it as our only reality. We hung the masks inside the tents and our future homes, taking the carnival with us. Unfortunately, the shamans took their roles very seriously, which eventually became their downfall.

After our stay in the mountains, we traveled to Aspen, Jackson Hole, and Laramie, hiking part of the Continental Divide. Then we journeyed east to Iowa and finally to New York City. We began to create seminars and evenings of instruction as a tribe. The seminars lasted from three to seven days and involved fasting, detoxifying the body, mask making, storytelling, teachings on the assemblage point, Vipassana meditation, the differentiation of male and female, and attunement to intuition, spirit guides, and totem animals.

During this time, Damien became more authoritarian. He drank a lot of wine, took ecstasy, blamed women for wars, and acted like a colonel in the air force. He began to relate stories of his past . . . He had gone bankrupt in New York; his fitness business had collapsed. Afterward, he had hitchhiked to California in a Scottish kilt. There, he had studied with various spiritual healers and teachers, practiced meditation, learned to communicate with various dimensions, and ended up at Mount Shasta, where, he said, he had been healed of his past wounds and exorcised of his demons. He had met Leah in Mill Valley, and shortly afterward they had had a simultaneous dream.

They had dreamt they were in a Mayan temple, walking

up a pyramid to be married in the jungle. They had both been spiritually initiated into the priestly orders, and both remembered incarnations as Mayan leaders. During the dream, their assemblage points had become active, and threads had emerged from their solar plexuses. Together, they had experienced a profound awakening, realizing they had a destiny to fulfill together. Later, they had received a loan from friends and had gone to Santa Fe to teach about the essence of male and female and to write a book together.

I felt Damien's wounded child, his alcoholic father, and his addiction to power. Once during this trip, he turned to me across a dining table and said, "You know I killed you as a priest in the Catholic Church. Do you forgive me? Can you trust me again? You were a killer, too. You have killer eyes."

Soon after that, Leah had black eyes again and vowed to leave Damien for good. Leah carried a deep sense of shame and abandonment from childhood but lacked a strong enough ego to confront her negative male side. The two of them played favorites, pitting the rest of us against each other. They promoted competition and sleep deprivation by keeping us up for hours playing a war game called Risk. Damien would often force us to play the board game all night—in order, he said, to expose our shadows, competitiveness, and our attachments to winning.

We gave up our power to Damien, and he began to fall apart. Dreams and memories came back to haunt him. He began acting out, both sexually with women in the group and with his fists. He came back one evening drunk, blaming Leah for not "moving the energies" in the seminars. He constantly blamed the feminine for the ills of war and for anything that went awry in a seminar, never taking responsibility for himself.

Arriving in New York, I felt I had come full circle. There, one night someone broke into our van, and I reexperienced all my childhood violation. The shamans began to tell me what to channel to audiences. They manipulated me to promote them, asking me to charge for my services and to give them a percentage of the profit. They urged me to recruit more and more people on the telephone at higher and higher prices.

Finally I had had enough. I packed my bags and waited by the apartment elevator, my heart racing. When the elevator arrived, Damien was in it. He got out, looked at my bags, and exploded. "Where do you think you're going? You owe us a lot of money for our time together. You owe us respect as your teachers. You will work for us until you have paid us back and we decide to let you go." He called me a lizard, but I knew that he was only projecting his own shadow onto me. (He and Leah were like the "Lizard People," the Nibiruans, who could not feel and who had controlled the Earth in a previous age.)

Damien took me back to my room and barred the door, threatening to call the police. "If you leave now, the ruthless tyrant will catch up to you," he said. "You must complete with us properly or you will drag these memories around all your life. You will thank me for this later."

I trembled as Damien screamed through me. None of my friends in the group supported me, not even Tani. At that moment, we became a dysfunctional cult. Tani started to act strangely, obsessed with darkness and her shadow self. She began to channel a demonic being.

Damien had become Wotan, the king of the gods in Teutonic mythology—the perfectionist father figure. Leah was Sieglinde, his daughter, taking care of her father's emotions, playing the surrogate wife. She gave up her own personality to become Damien's anima. There were days when no one was home in Leah's body, and she often had an eerie smile on her face. When Leah behaved contrary to Damien's emotional expectations, he gave her a black eye. One night, I even saw him beating her up and climbed on his back to make him stop.

At Jenny Lake in the Grand Teton Mountains, I had hit my forehead on a shower head, and a bluish, bulbous protrusion had formed at the point of my third eye. After that, I started to see through my pituitary gland. My perceptions altered dramatically. I saw Damien and Leah's past lives, including their murders of each other by poisoning and their abuses of power. I also saw how they had victimized me over and over in past lifetimes. This was the beginning of the end of my collusion with tyranny.

In the days following our confrontation at the elevator, Damien was irritable and upset with me. I looked deep into his body at his demons. I looked right through him, and he began to feel uncomfortable, unsafe. He could not control me anymore. I no longer chose to be either victim or victimizer.

Was I violating Damien by looking so deeply into his being? Owls flew over my head, telling me to see in the dark, to expose his and my own weaknesses, and to redeem the wounded man in both of us. Damien tried to battle me in dreams, still needing to dominate me and make me his servant. I said, "No, Damien. I am stronger now. The game is over."

The only book I had that dealt with the ruthless tyrant was Carlos Castaneda's *The Fire Within*. I began to plot out various strategies to leave the group. Damien and Leah reminded me that I owed them $2,500 for apprenticing with them and that I had signed a document to that effect. They threatened to take me to court if I left the group prematurely. Damien and Leah complained on and on about my lack of integrity, the dishonoring of my teachers, and my betrayal of them.

I was not going to be trapped. I called all my old friends asking for money, but no one offered to help. Finally, my father sent me a plane ticket to Los Angeles to spend Christmas with my family. This, I realized, was my way out.

On the winter solstice, we arranged a big celebration. I channeled on the need to be heard and touched, and on the birth of true values and maturity. I was lecturing to the shamans to live their talk. In return, Damien and Leah carefully devised a binding ceremony in which they asked all of us to dedicate ourselves to their service for a year.

I played along, knowing they were cording themselves to my solar plexus and trying to trap my life force. Tani, the filmmaker, and two others stayed with the shamans, vowing allegiance, and new recruits joined in to be their apprentices. In the days that followed, I felt them weaving strange cocoons around my body. They began to alter my assemblage point and gave me war medals as a sign of my allegiance to them. Strangers came up to me asking why I was with these people, and I told them point blank: "This is my shadow, the shadow of control and manipulation. I am going to face it head-on and be empowered. Then I will get out of here and learn to act from my gut as a man."

I left for Los Angeles. There, I saw Rianna again and my feelings began to unravel. I decorded my solar plexus, distancing myself emotionally, and cried for days, releasing the shamans' binding spells. I even wrote them a "channeled" message from a "master" acknowledging their contribution to my life, telling them what they wanted to hear, admitting that I had been their apprentice and that now was the time to move on. I set up a payment schedule—anything to free my soul from its Faustian pact. A friend in the film world had mentioned a possible job, so I included that in the letter, trying to cover all my tracks.

It worked. The shamans would be paid and honored. A woman outside the group in New York, an actress I will call Helen, offered me money so that I could pay the shamans immediately and leave them. I accepted, and this, too, eventually became a great teaching. Helen said she found Damien abusive and Leah teetering on the brink of madness. Meanwhile, I forgave myself and mentally reviewed the previous six months for the lessons they had taught me about giving my power away. I even loved Damien and Leah for teaching me not to act from emotional and financial greed.

I wanted to make peace. I wanted to have boundaries, the personal boundaries I had never had as a child. I wanted to heal my animus, the man who had excluded women in his life and was controlled by a negative mother and an authoritarian, perfectionist father.

During this time, I had dreams about America. I saw how American citizens would eventually lose their rights, beginning with search-and-seizure practices. I saw how both Democrats and Republicans were loyal to a growing military-industrial complex and how tax monies were filtered to defense contractors and Pentagon officials. In these dreams, I even received the names of the 1 percent of American society that controlled the wealth and cared little for the common person. Voting had become an act of theater. America would be safe only for money, not for people. Not since

Atlantis had the public and the media become so completely
brainwashed.

I was told in my dreams to be skeptical of television,
politicians, and the military. I journeyed in visions to underground military installations in Australia and Sedona,
Arizona. I did not like what I saw. The technology was
dangerous. The work with photons and genetics was abhor-
rent to life. I saw lots of military personnel in Las Vegas,
Nevada, flying metallic spaceships made by the government.
Then I saw Reptile People walking around.

This was deep dreaming of events to come that had
already been set into motion; however, I did not take the
dreams literally or become paranoid. I also saw hope in these
visions—hope for massive social and spiritual revolution.
Change was coming from within, and I knew I must remain
true to my own soul.

I returned to New York to pack my bags and say good-
bye to the shamans, Tani, and two others of the group. The
shamans cried and took me out to lunch. Then they told me
that in addition to the money I had already paid them, I had
to tithe to them in Los Angeles. According to their schedule,
I would practically have to tithe to them for the rest of my
life. Their plan was outrageous, but I bit my tongue, waiting
for the right moment to make my break. I remembered our
time in the mountains and inwardly forgave them, but I
wanted them out of my hair. On the last day, they cut my
long hair, releasing the past. I had always associated the
cutting of hair not only with a release of the past but also
with the loss of power.

Through Damien and Leah, I had seen the dynamics of
my family dysfunction in the clearest possible mirror. My

father had been a powerful leader who had demanded perfection in school and sports and had always seemed to know
what was "right." My mother had suppressed her feelings,
becoming a manic-depressive who was addicted to drugs like
Valium, Librium, and Thorazine.

My father had once told me, "You are emotional like your
mother. It's a genetic condition that runs in her side of the
family." He had a fixation on logic and knowledge. He was
adored at work but not intimate at home. My mother went
mad for a while in her manic depression. She lost her soul to
the inner tyrant of patriarchy, the shadow side of my father
that could not feel. She stayed in bed for almost a year, not
wanting to face life.

I was my parents' go-between, caught up in their web,
because I loved and needed them so much as a child. I had
seen my father judge everyone yet want us to adore him and
live near him when we grew up. Nothing my mother did
was enough for him. He was a Taurus who wanted to be
loved but could not let his family go. At an early age, I had
refused to take care of my mother's emotional needs. I had
learned how to be independent of her, even though it had
caused me great pain.

Like my father had done, Damien would not let me go.
He thought his attachments to me were strings of love. He
believed I was a son longing for my father's return and that
I could find these things through him. It was true that I
wanted to bond with the positive potential in Damien, but
I also needed to protect myself against his suppression of
soul and feeling and his bouts of intense rage. I had to
discover my own shadow, not take on his.

As I thought about it, I realized that both Damien and
my father were walking a fine line between the drive for

power and the instinct for self-preservation. Both of them projected an unintegrated masculine side, a brutal shadow egoism. While thus analyzing Damien and my father, I realized that it was important for me to acknowledge and love not only my good side but also my inferior side. Now was the time to descend into the underworld to face the things that had always held me back.

Meanwhile, the shamans called my job contacts in Los Angeles and found out that I was not working for a film company after all. They felt betrayed and demanded more weekly money.

Hearing this, I broke off all communications and tore up all my agreements with them. To me, real masculinity had always meant a kind of forcefulness that said, *"I want that; I am going to have that."* I tore out the shamans' psychic cords and discarded all my dependencies on them. I took a stand as a man and said, simply, "No!" Never again did I allow them to contact me, write me letters, or demand money. I was their apprentice no more. After months of disentangling my soul, studying John Bradshaw's work on family systems, I felt free and much stronger.

My first week in Los Angeles I landed a job acting in commercials: "We love the Sprite in you." My guides were telling me something. Sitting by the ocean, I became more relaxed, breathing out the experiences of the last six months, grieving my broken heart that would open again in time.

Helen, the actress who had given me the money to leave the shamans, flew to Los Angeles to share a house with me in Topanga Canyon. She wanted to sleep in the same room and mother me. She was Greek and manic-depressive, and she wanted to bond with me as her lover. Thus, she became the mirror of my childhood relationship with my mother.

I had loved my mother as a child. We were inseparable. When I was three, she took me away from my father to meet her family in Greece. I spoke fluent Greek, lived with my aunt and grandparents, and remembered my past lives there. My mother and I experienced great joy together in Greece. We played in the royal gardens, laughed, ate luscious meals, and enjoyed feeling like a family.

When we returned to my father and siblings, though, a terrible break occurred. My father wanted me to separate from my mother and pursue sports. I was only four years old. My mother became crazy. She felt guilty for smothering me but dared not cross him. They fought constantly.

It was then that she began to take a great many prescription pills. She longed for Greece, her homeland, her language, her family and friends, but she didn't have the strength to leave. She was torn between these things and the wealth and prestige my father offered. So she escaped into an inner world. I wanted her attention again, but she was far away, often outside her body. Sometimes she came to me in dreams as her true self, as an ancient healer, my Greek sister.

I dearly loved my mother's sister, my aunt Anastasia. She was earthy, outspoken, nurturing, and independent. I prayed that my mother would discover that she was more like Anastasia than she realized.

When Helen the Greek actress arrived, I knew life would become difficult and that I would have to make a conscious break with my mother. Helen and I were playing roles, and I was grateful for her lessons. She was a dramatic actress who wanted to be my whole world. She demanded attention, healing, and constant love, just like my mother had. She wanted me to take care of her and live her dream of me as her lover/son.

I became emotionally detached, telling her I could not share a room with her. She called me the devil for luring her back to Los Angeles, which she had left to pursue an acting career in New York, and taking her money. I worked diligently at my job, rarely seeing her, and paid her back all her money. I told her I didn't want to have a relationship with her. She packed her bags and cursed me for using her.

In Helen, I recognized the wounded, rejected feminine in myself. Focusing inward, dialoguing with my own inner woman, I started to release my mother's patterns. I became more aware of the judgmental man within me, the inner critic. I slowed down, healing myself through introversion and solitude. Seeing the shadow and learning when to engage it and when to establish clear boundaries was the work of the next few years.

EIGHT

JOURNEY TO THE UNDERWORLD

*J*ungian dreamwork helped to prepare me for the next stage of my journey. A year after leaving the shamans, I had a powerful dream:

My mother and I are standing in the backyard of my childhood home, looking at the swimming pool. There has just been a violent storm, and leaves and branches have been tossed all over the yard and the pool. It is lush and wild, like the unconscious.

A giant turtle walks past my mother and jumps into the pool. I turn to my mother and say, "You are no longer my mother. I will not stay home with you anymore. I break from you. The Earth is my mother now."

I walk toward the pool and dive in. The turtle swims directly toward me. It is massive. I touch the design on its shell. Then I swim under the turtle's belly, sheltered, protected under the water.

My physical mother was not the archetypal Mother. With this dream, a transference of energy had begun to the turtle, to Mother Earth, and I felt safe beneath her. I had to break from my physical mother, to cease looking through

her eyes at my father and judging him. It was time for me
to become a steward of the Earth.

Nurturing the colors of the inner male was the key. During a visit to Taos, on a windy fall night, I had the following
dream:

*I am carrying milk bottles with nipples on the path from my
childhood home to the peacock cage. The peacocks are malnourished
and about to die. I feed them the milk, staying with them until
they become plump and glowing with life. When they are spar-
kling with color and I feel they can be on their own, I leave them,
following the path back to my parents' house.*

*It is fall, and leaves cover the ground. In the leaves I see a
baby elephant rolling on its back. We become friends, playing
together, rolling in the yellow leaves. Then I think about mother
elephants, which are very protective of their young. I realize the
mother elephant will kill me if she finds me playing here.*

*Suddenly, the mother elephant arrives, and she is alarmed.
Instead of running, though, I continue playing—laughing and
feeding her baby. Her mood changes when she sees how joyful we
are together and how well I have taken care of her child. She
accepts me as part of her family. After that, I leave my parents'
home and go to live with the elephants.*

This was a dream about nurturing different aspects of
myself, like the colors of the peacock. It was time to show
my colors. In my dream, I had found a new, instinctual inner
family that could truly love me with the proverbial elephant
wisdom.

I try not to analyze dreams but instead to stay with the
images. By keeping the images inside or painting and writing about them, they tend to gather numinosity and meaning. In this way, the images reverberate at deeper levels

of recognition that are often robbed by interpretation. Staying with the image brings depth of feeling and eventual integration.

As I mentioned, when I was a child my father kept Mandarin ducks in a large aviary. When they interbred, they sometimes produced offspring that were blind. One night, I went to the duck cage and sat very still. The seeing ducks avoided me, but one blind duck, navigating on feeling, eventually found its way to my lap and sat there. I felt I was that blind duck, different from the collective, a kind of genetic blindness murmuring in my blood. I stayed up all night stroking the duck, feeling the wounds of my childhood.

As an adult, I returned to those cages to heal my soul through dreams:

I am a bird in my father's aviaries. My father and mother are outside looking in at me. After many days, my father opens the cage door—first a little, then all the way. I do not know if it is safe to leave.

One day, my parents leave, and the door is wide open. I turn into a bluebird and fly out, my soul free. I never have to return again.

My soul had to be set free to discover the natural world. The bluebird of happiness—the image of my soul—took flight. It was my inner parents who gave me permission. Later, when my parents moved from my boyhood home, they actually did set the remaining birds free. After my dream, a woman came over to my house and left me an empty bird cage with a nest inside. The door always remained open.

When I moved back to Santa Fe in 1988 to experience my Saturn Return—the time of discipline, responsibilities, and finding one's vocation—a bluebird came. The bird kept

hitting the windows of my house, fighting its reflection in
the glass. Its testosterone level was high, and it was battling
itself as the enemy. For days, as I began to give healing sessions, the bluebird knocked itself into the windows. I ran
outside shooing it away, but it always returned within a few
minutes.

Finally I went outside to talk to the bird. It told me I was
fighting the image of myself, the mirror of my masculinity. I
had to stop dueling the man inside, the reflection of my soul.
I must break the mirror of collective normalcy and integrate
my shadow.

The next day, the bluebird built a nest in the mailbox.
It had given me the lesson of my new home and my future
work. It had told me I would help men and women face their
destructive Sethian animus, their warlike shadow, and transform it into creative fire.

Around that time, I received a phone invitation from a
woman friend to go to Bimini in the Bahamas and swim with
the dolphins. For a long time I had communicated with dolphins telepathically and heard their messages of rebirth, but
I had never been around them physically. Now it was time to
dive into the unconscious and hear what they had to tell me
at closer range.

Bimini consists of two islands sixty miles west of Miami.
This is the place where Atlantis is said to be buried. At sea
level, I felt dense, warm, subterranean. Dreams of the underworld filled my psyche. I wanted to be where the mountain
streams gather in the valleys. Each day, my friend and I
stayed in the water, snorkeling, diving, letting the ocean
support us. It was like being in a womb.

We had come to Bimini to touch the memories of
Atlantis and communicate with the etheric Bimini Pyra-

mid. We relaxed in radon-filled pools, went to the supposed fountain of youth, and touched the ruins of an Atlantean wall. We meditated, read books, dreamed, and talked to the Atlantean gatekeepers.

We began to remember that we had been dolphins in other lives. We had also worked in a temple in Atlantis, speaking to dolphins, learning about life in the pod. While in Bimini, I heard a legend about golden dolphins—of how their consciousness permeated humankind. The constellation Delphinius was one of our homes, a place of rest, introversion, and delight.

When my friend and I swam with the dolphins, both in captivity and in the wild, they caressed our bodies, echolating through our cellular membranes. Echolation is the incredible experience of dolphins vibrating, singing, breathing through one's whole body. They bombard you with sensory impressions, creating walls of holographic sound-pictures. They are also very sensual creatures. They nuzzle your chest and thighs, breathe sounds through the pores of your skin, even alter your heartbeat. Being in their presence, you learn not to fear the water but instead to surrender to the spirit of playfulness.

My waking mind was overwhelmed by my experience with the dolphins, and it took a long time to recover. Long after I had returned to Santa Fe, I kept receiving subconscious imprints from the dolphins. Images of descent— into the unconscious, the underworld—flashed before my eyes. It was then that I started to die. I simply gave up living. Intense pain grew in my lymph system, like a cancer eating away at me. I could no longer work. I felt listless, paralyzed.

All my guides seemed to have vanished. I asked for a miracle, but nothing happened. I felt that a boat was coming to take me away. I wanted to be in the water, free like a dolphin. What had the dolphins done to activate this? I had no answers, only waves of tears. I cried for weeks. I felt completely blank, as though I knew nothing. Somehow, I had to return to the dolphins.

This was my dark night of the soul. Years of extroverted activity passed before my eyes like waking dreams. I saw Whale Rock in Topanga Canyon outside Los Angeles, a sacred site within walking distance of my former home. I had sat in caves there, talking to the Record Keepers of the Earth's stories. I had seen ships from other worlds that were organic, alive, like viruses floating in space. I had cried when I saw how no one was picking up the litter there. People no longer respected the sacredness of the place. Houses were being built right next to it. Had I failed in my duty to surround it with love?

I saw Joshua Tree and all the nights I had stayed there in the rock temples, talking to the stars, learning the constellations, seeing reptilian beings. They had been friendly, saying they were returning from the twelfth planet in the Solar System. Many of them had incarnated in human bodies in previous epochs. "Follow joy" was their message. "Do not be as controlling as we once were."

I perceived faces of hundreds of famous people: writers, artists, friends I had worked with in Los Angeles. Was I completing my stay there? I saw Bay Island, a haven for millionaires off the coast of Newport Beach. A friend from Aspen had wanted me to retreat to her home there and write a book. I read about dysfunctional family systems and mother complexes and found solitude in the poetry of Rumi and Rilke, watching doves birthing their young outside my bedroom window. This was a key step toward my return to Santa Fe.

Then I began to flash on the last few months: trips to
Hawaii, bathing in waterfalls, witnessing kahunas reverse
lava flows. I remembered how Pele, the Hawaiian goddess
of fire and fertility, had stroked my neck, telling me of her
lovers, the volcanoes, and her homes on the Pleiades and in
the volcanoes on the island of Hawaii. I had bathed in secret
pools on Maui and descended into Haleakala Crater on the
old kahuna path. My chakras had burst open at the bottom
of the huge valley; Haleakala was a gateway to Inner Earth.

White owls had circled there, messengers of the Dreamtime. Kahunas said that silver flowers from the Pleiades grew
in this valley. A Tibetan lama on Maui had embraced my
girlfriend and me, touching and holding us. The other people were amazed. They had never seen him touch anyone.
We had meditated in a sanctuary on the crystal path of
Dzogchen, the Tibetan Buddhist practice of clarity and
transcendence. We had felt the presence of the female
deities—the *dakinis*—and the women of protection and
learning. We had been surrounded by great love.

Had all this been a preparation for my descent into the
underworld? My longtime artist friend Mirtala flashed before
me, making sculptures in red rock, communicating with
angels and devas. We had been traveling together, driving on
the freeway in Albany, New York. All of a sudden, time had
shifted and we were on the other side of the road, traveling
in the opposite direction. We had gotten our bearings and
driven off the freeway at the first exit. As we drove back
toward Albany, a huge rainbow had appeared over the road.
We would have missed it had we not been diverted.

I saw myself enter the underworld. A boatman gestured
me to come, then I saw the River Styx. I saw the last memories of my earthly life being reviewed, including all the

people to whom I had given readings and guidance. I felt
them receiving empowerment and joy. Thousands of people
had touched my short life. The sense of community was
overwhelming.

Now the waters in my veins were returning to their
source. Creation seemed to dissolve into pure light. I became
more and more transparent. I saw the shamans smiling. They
told me my experience with them was a rite of passage from
a boy to a man, as in a tribal community, to teach me to take
responsibility for my actions. I did not have to judge them
any longer for what they had done. In that long moment, I
thanked them and forgave them, then forgave myself. This
was the last judgment, my inner reckoning.

Spiraling downward, all my sexual fantasies swirled in
my brain. I saw a gay man and a heterosexual man walking
as brothers down a street, celebrating their differences. I
heard a narrator say, "It's glorious being a man, and you do
not need to label your sexuality. It is the purpose of manhood
to love your brother and defend his rights. Release your
homophobia and be heard. Men will gather in groups soon to
form a circle of knowing. Men will learn to nurture and love
one another again.

"Hear the instructions of original Creation and reach out
your hand to your father," the voice went on. "This journey
is for you both. Love and embrace him. It is the end of your
karmic past together. He was once your lover when you were
a woman. He was a powerful man in Atlantis. In Bimini you
released your fixed memories and judgments of him. Your
father is now free to go through his own transformation."

The inner voice prepared me later for the men's work I
would do. It was a call to the wild, feeling man inside. As I
began to sink deeper into death, I saw Krishnamurti's face.

He loved me like a son. He was leaving his body, having spasms, his pancreas in pain. He took my hand and told me, "Do not be bitter. We are all world teachers. Watch your mind, but feel also, and have a human, sensitive life." My face became pale and expressionless as he said the last few words. I wanted to find the gifts in this depression.

As I released that thought, I saw myself as an Egyptian temple dancer, dancing the movements of the stars. A priest and priestess prepared my body for the underworld journey. They gave me snakes to hold, and the snakes bit my arms. This would bring visions.

I saw my descent through mythic stories. I saw that Mary Magdalene was a priestess in Egypt, and I witnessed her preparing for her descent to marry Christ. I saw Sumerian king Gilgamesh descending to find his friend Enkidu, who had died defending him. I realized that this was a conscious initiation for a purpose: to redeem my soul and the soul of my father.

I was greeted by Anubis, the jackal-headed dog who conducts the dead to judgment. Dogs and jackals stared at me in silence, letting me pass into an inner sanctum. I gave the ferryman coins. He took me to a gondola. We floated effortlessly on the golden water.

Massive sculptures were falling in ruins as we passed by. I saw columns submerged in the thick golden water below the boat. We were going to an island. I thought of the fairy lady in Tennyson's poem "The Lady of Shallot," passing Camelot in her boat as she died. I saw the Tor in the distance to remind me I had taken this journey many times before.

Inanna, the Sumerian goddess, took off my clothes when we arrived. She said I would dance fourteen veils, not seven. She began to take off my bodies, initiating me into both male and female mysteries. My skin tore off. I was naked and glowing like a ball of golden light. I felt contained and self-sufficient. Pluto, Greek god of the underworld, came up to me and touched my shoulder, and I felt a cold transformation taking place. Tarot images lined the walls of the temple—or was it a mausoleum? I heard dervishes whirling in side rooms in perfect circles.

Then Pluto turned to me and said, "I have come to show you Osiris's body. This will be your next work. You are here in the land of the midnight sun. That sun will rise in you now. As above, so below. Look at Ren, the inner meaning of names. Thoth will teach your heart more mysteries of Ren. Give up the magic, the shamanism, and join a community of like-minded souls. Your life will go beyond the past, beyond initiations, to a group consciousness. With others you may share humility and respect for humankind and know each other equally. You have prepared a long time in other lives for this moment."

I saw the mountains of the underworld. I had come here for gold—for lessons in rejuvenating the body, transforming cells, tissue, the astral body. Eventually, there would be great rejuvenation centers on Earth and communities of healers.

"Slow down," a voice said. I felt roots sinking deep into one mountain to the center of the Earth. I heard a list of the lessons of initiatic activity: facing the shadow, learning multidimensionality without fragmenting the psyche, breaking free from the Solar System in the light body, passing through the time-space continuum easily and with discernment, seeing essence as identity, shapeshifting, knowing and relating to the angels and devas, and so on.

I saw humankind being initiated in dreams, to dream a new world through children and conscious adults. Every-

thing on Earth was becoming translucent, the divine showing clearly through our mundane lives. I saw how comets
would alarm the Earth, causing great change. I saw how a
bright blue star would shine in the sky in A.D. 2012. The
new millennium would be filled with surprises: Earth movements, a return to traditional ways, and a greatly increased
capacity for light in our physical bodies.

I heard through my heart: "You are clearing the past and
future as one. There is no time. The psyche is being healed
through widening its base. Welcome Osiris, the sun. He is
the man being born in you."

Then I was shown a holographic play. Osiris stood before
me. He was tricked into entering a coffin, killed, torn apart,
and pieces of him scattered like corn. Isis and Thoth rear-
ranged the pieces, bringing him down to the underworld.

I then saw the birth of Horus and a generation of sons
returning to redeem their fathers. I saw Horus defeat Seth,
his inner beast, and redeem his shadow. Then I saw Osiris
return to life and embrace his son. Proudly he turned to face
me. He held my hand, and a sun rose into my soul. He
walked into my body, and I became a hologram of the god
himself.

After this ritual, I was dazed. I did not understand it
yet but felt changed. I did not know how this would affect
my daily life. Who were Osiris and Horus? Why had they
appeared to me? What was the message to impart to others?
Then I saw my higher self in a coffin, dead. I realized I was
lost without her. In grief, I dismembered my body, surrendering my ego. My blood spilled on the garments of my
higher self, resurrecting her. She sewed me back together
in a new way, as a new man.

I rose out of the underworld like the Aurora Borealis, the

aura of the Earth, and journeyed from Inner Earth through the North Pole to Alcyone in the Pleiades. I made the trip easily in a brand new body, shimmering.

Then I found myself in an amphitheater that looked like a giant seashell. A holographic image was displayed there for all to see: the image of a phoenix rising from the ashes, fire burning from its eyes and wings.

I asked a woman near me, "What does this mean?" She smiled and said, "You are being reborn. You can return to the stars now. Face the bull."

The bull was the Pleiades. Now a hologram of a bull stood before me, and I became a participant in the drama. I faced a Cretan maze, a labyrinth of the mind. I knew the bull was a hologram, and I was not afraid. I touched the bull's head and horns, then caressed its body. It devoured me whole. My body was filled with light. Then I heard, "The bull is your father. You and the father will become one. You can return home with an open heart now to the Fifth World, the World of Flowers."

Then Raven, Owl, Elk, Dolphin, Frog, Armadillo—all my totem animals—came to retrieve me. "The World of Flowers is the opening of your heart in great love and compassion," the voice said. I saw the midnight sun rise and send rays through my body. I became like that sun, light radiating from my form. My animal guides took me back to the center crystal inside the Earth, and I saw my diamond body receive another facet. I was shining with a new armor, silvery and translucent. I was the sun, and the sun was in me.

Holding a diamond in my palm, I was gently thrust back into my body lying on a bed. The room seemed the same. I was soaked in sweat and had a very high fever. My homeopath sat next to me, administering remedies. "You don't look so good. I thought I had lost you just then."

I had died from a high fever. How long had I been gone? Three days? Three hours? Why did I remember it all so vividly? I heard my intuition speaking to me: "You have made friends with your brother, Death, the dark lord. You have returned to teach something. We had to give you the teaching whole. Live simply now. The drama is over. Your recovery will be swift."

Gratitude filled my aching body. I thanked the stars, Grandmother Earth, Grandfather Sky, the dolphins, my allies, and even Death, now a friend.

I told no one what I had gone through. It was essential to keep it inside, build an inner strength, and not give the visions away too quickly. Each day, as I recovered, I imagined sending roots deeper and deeper into the soil, into the psyche. I felt as though I were covered with earth, mud, and leaves. My body felt more solid and compact, my bones bigger and more supportive.

My soul said, "You have lifted the fourteen veils of Osiris, revealing your divine self. Share this with others and be part of a later community." I plunged into work and friendships with a new zeal for life.

I began to make drums and rattles. I saw grandmothers and grandfathers next to me as I worked, giving instruction. I collected hundreds of feathers, stones from anthills, and talked to the Ant People. They said, "Spirits now fill your home, and they are wise, benevolent allies. Keep the fires going. Let them burn brightly for all to see."

Work changed dramatically. My voice deepened, filled with authority. I began to lead people in death and birth rituals. I had clients breathe in a circular pattern for two hours as I performed bodywork on them, realigning their meridians. I sang through the fibers of their assemblage points, moving the energies like a stream back to their source. Techniques for sound healing came to me as I investigated each person's body.

After intense bodywork and clearing of old patterns coupled with deep breathing, many people rebirthed themselves. I held their chests as they went into contractions. After the birth process was complete, I led them into death. I mummified their bodies in blankets, sheets, and towels. When their breath slowed down and I felt them journeying, I sang. I sang the songs I heard during my own near-death experience. As the last song ended, I unrolled the garments. The fourteen veils were lifted, and each person was reborn.

People wept in my arms, feeling full and empty, deeply cleansed for the first time in their lives. With eyes wide open, they looked like children. I reintroduced them to the Earth and sat them down near a medicine wheel.

A second form of work developed. I took people through their own soul records to complete the holograms of the past. For six hours, people read their own Akashic Records. I prepared them by visualizing the opening of their pineal gland and third eye and placing a triangle there. Then I cleared all the chakras and let them remain in their bodies while they journeyed.

During these journeys, people saw their past lives, why they had come to Earth, and their futures in this life and the next one. We traveled back to their creation at the beginning of time, where they connected to their higher selves as well as their middle and lower selves, guides, and teachers. Many visited states of consciousness between incarnations. I imagined their DNA changing from a two-strand helix to a twelve-strand and more. Everyone felt eternity, a fusion with the future, and the connections between dreams and all living things.

Hundreds of souls began to show up for these sessions. Many were advanced in visual perception, while others were beginners. I felt privileged and trusted. My home became filled with gifts. I created nineteen altars and numerous shrines and medicine wheels. Many people flew in from around the world. I had to concentrate on remaining clear, centered, simple, ordinary.

Ren, an Egyptian science of using a person's name to discover an aspect of their soul, became my course of study. Gaelic, Sanskrit, runic lore, mythic names, and genealogies became my area of scholarship. I listened for stories and the depths of a people's souls in their names. For three hours, I gave individual sessions based solely on the meanings of names.

During these sessions, through poetry, notes, and deep questioning, we pondered the meaning of our lives, sharing a great intimacy. The storyteller, healer, leader in everyone emerged like an artist. All my life experience was shared soul to soul, body to body, and broke through my clients' resistance to merging with the self. It was rewarding work, and I felt called and well prepared to do it.

Then came the giveaway. I could not charge for my work but was compensated generously for it anyway. It was important to live the example and not talk too much. I learned to live in a silence beyond death.

PART TWO

TEACHINGS

CANCER

A month after my near death, I received
a phone call about my father. He had been diagnosed with
cancer and would begin chemotherapy shortly. Just like myself in the midst of my Saturn Return, my father was going
through a transformation. Saturn represents discipline,
structure, law. The structures of the masculine in both our
lives were changing simultaneously. This was my father's
final karmic gift to me.

I wanted to listen to the cancer cells in my father's body
and understand the origins of his disease. I imagined entering my genetic bloodline, the ancestral memories of the past
to find and understand the roots of cancer. As I did so, the
disease itself began to speak to me. I learned that cancer is
created by not feeling. Cancer takes root when we follow an
outside authority or believe that we are our work. In a nine-
to-five mentality, the life of the soul loses precedence to
the collective mind. But as the light resonance in our body
develops, the old ideas of work and identity must change.
Cancer is telling us to slow down, stop working, and bring
feeling, caring, and nourishment into the body.

How can this be done? First, we need to release the belief
that we are not our emotions. Emotion is a true barometer
of the inner life that is being suppressed. Then we need to
transform our work into compassionate service. We may have
given away our essence to a work ethic, an organization, or a
collective belief that is obsolete. Our soul may be trying to
slow us down so that we will appreciate life and feel the grief
of the past and the eventual freedom of self-love.

The destruction of tissues and the loss of protective fields
around the body are produced by fear. When fear sets in, we
forget that we are always protected. We lose the feeling of
being an integral part of creation. We forget to love our
bodies and the beauty and simplicity of being human. Sometimes this stems from birth, when a mother is unable to nurture a baby because of her own fears.

I remember my own mother's anxiety at my birth—
racing to the hospital a half hour away, pushing me back into
the womb until she was ready to birth me. I remember the
slap, the gasping for air, and being whisked to a laboratory
room where a plastic sucking tube was thrust into my
mouth. I felt no contact with my mother, no warm breast,
no gradual immersion in water, no safety. Life was fast, un-
feelingly cruel, and antiseptic. Births like this are profound
betrayals of a child's soul.

The belief instilled in my soul at birth was that life was
a fight for survival: thrust, ram, rush, without reflection or
introspection. I had to stay erect, rigid, and not breathe too
deeply for whatever might come. The idea was to control life
to prevent a scarcity of money, food, and love.

The mythological Greek king Oedipus had to lose his
eyes in order to gain insight. We need to acknowledge our
feelings and all the pain we suppress through reason and

intellect. In cancer, we must learn to surrender to a larger perspective—to a transformation and empowerment of that abandoned child whose soul was not seen or celebrated.

Our need to control life destroys the integrity of our cells, making them fight and ravage us. The manipulation of others in order to feel is the wrong use of will and has caused infinite damage to our individual spirits. We human beings have become addicted to suffering. Suffering is one of the few ways we can access feeling today.

But there is another way to feel: through intimate relationship to our own bodies and each other. For men, this is a relatedness with the creative masculine as Eros. Women must find their buried creativity and allow themselves to feel beautiful, sensual, impulsive, living their own life force in action. Rainer Maria Rilke says that the connection of one human being to another has no model, no path laid out. We must risk opening to other human beings with consistency, vulnerability, and the intimate lessons of our wounds.

When we open to the pain inside ourselves, it is the same as giving birth. Life is relationship. Our wounds contain all the creativity, feelings, thoughts, and dreams we never acted on. Form a relationship with your cancer. Talk to it. Ask it why it is screaming for attention. Love your wound. Kiss it and nurture it back to health.

Our perfectionism judges our wounds too harshly in this society. We need to stop putting ourselves on trial. Cancer is an opportunity to fill ourselves with love and not feel like outcasts or that something is wrong with us. It is a time to enter the fold of real human values based on a loving society.

Our perfectionism is mirrored in our judgmental religions and in an amazing array of laws and restrictions. We all feel a loss of liberty and self when too many laws violate our lives. Cancer is a time to stop and look at our belief systems of sin, unworthiness, and judgment. No one really judges us but ourselves. We are not unworthy; we are all greatly loved by this Earth.

The center of the Earth is pristine and can never be penetrated by the violence of our thoughts or actions. It is an untouched garden. When we surrender in the experience of cancer, we are invited to the center of that garden to witness our own birth and our inclusion in creation. She asks us to surrender to a new perspective on life, one that is nurturing to the soul.

Radiation is the bombardment of a cell with massive doses of light. Imagine that radiation is a gift of light. Before chemotherapy, meditate. Imagine your cancer enveloped by color, love, and acceptance. Make friends with your disease. Give it the care you may have never given yourself. Draw pictures of the disease in your body getting smaller and less dark Give your wounds a voice.

The goal of cancer is self-love. The quest is to unite the opposites within us, the inner male and female. Stop the internal chatter of your parents' voices. Relive parts of your past to find out what is the *unlived essence* in you. End the past and get a life. Life is a unity of soul and spirit. Cancer is a call to become deeply spiritual, to see through our souls to the wonder of the world around us.

Honor the Earth again. Greet the sun when it rises. Believe that you make a difference on this planet. We have all created our own reality, and we can all heal ourselves. Believe in yourself. Learn tools of visualization. Find a joyful form of meditation. Learn how to live fully again.

Do not believe doctors when they pronounce you terminal. Prove them wrong. The power of mind and feeling can cure cancer completely. Never believe anyone if they have a negative thought about your condition. Create your own world of healing and act accordingly.

Aggression is healthy, and it is good to honor your desires; they are the life force. Face the ruthless tyrant, aggression turned inward, and break the mirror. Realize your aggression as a desire to serve, be outspoken, play when you want to, and nurture your body into flexibility.

Before my eyes, my father was transformed from a rigid authoritarian to a gentle, sensitive man. His hair fell out, and he lost dozens of pounds. He became humble, meek, adaptive, and kind. He faced his mortality. My father's baldness was the symbol of the reborn child. He sacrificed himself and his intellectual thoughts and went through a rebirth in his own underworld. He became the sun, a child of God, a child of the Goddess, in the quest to retrieve his soul.

Christ's only wound was that he was human. He was the essence of the Wounded Healer archetype. Chiron, a planetesimal asteroid or comet discovered in 1977, symbolizes how we must embrace and endure our wounds like Christ in order to become healers of the soul. When we explore our wounds to heal them, then that becomes our ministry, our next work. My father was a doctor who needed to heal himself.

The Latin root of the word *vulnerable* means "wound." God comes through our wounds, our vulnerability. Being vulnerable is our strength. Opening to a place of humility and humanness exposes our wounds to love. The wound is where our genius lies. Cancer is a call to find God, our creativity, and our untapped genius.

No matter how much pain you are in, your wounds call out for the salt of the Earth to heal it. Let go of the vertical path to God and seek the horizontal path of the heart. Be in the expanse of the vast, embracing plains, seeing through your heart a hundred miles in all directions. Lick your wounds like an animal. Let the salt of blood, sweat, and tears lead you to a more expanded view of humanity.

Above all, do not play victim to your disease—after all, you created it. Instead, learn that you can heal yourself. Remember that it is a call to end old habits of shame and blame. Find the wisdom in the wound.

Fear is the opposite of love. Fear is outside you and does not have to be internalized. It is the great illusion of human-kind that fear has power over love. At the end of a black hole is often a white hole. There is great light at the end of the cancer tunnel. Light is supporting you to change.

Shatter the mirror of how you are supposed to deal with fear or anger and how you are supposed to be polite and nice. You may have been taught to hold in a profound aggression or profoundly healthy anger. The soul keeps all the pain we try to suppress. We must heal our self-abuse, stop being so nice, feel and express from the deepest well of our being.

Break the mirror of how others see you. People fix impressions of us with their eyes and do not release them, expecting us always to act and be the same. See a person's soul, their life force, not a stereotype. Release the ways you have behaved in the past. Know that cancer is a purification, a wiping the slate clean. Also know that no one is separate from you. When you look at another person, see another yourself. That person outside you needs your love. Stop seeing through your wounds.

I used to visit my parents, dreading the worst. All the old patterns of not relating would rear their ugly heads. The same emotional charges and disagreements would come up again and again. One day, I chose to stop and witness the patterns as they came up. Then I responded differently. As my father yelled, I lowered my voice, went into my soul, and spoke calmly to his soul. He did not have to expose my faults and insecurities in order to have a conversation. I chose to be spontaneous, a holy fool.

I loved my parents unconditionally, no matter what had happened in the past. It did not have to influence this moment. I felt their higher selves, and we did not have to change each other. Intimacy became the value to cherish. I learned to love my parents as they were. Transformation came from putting intimacy first.

I could not heal my father, but I prayed for him and talked to his soul and his cancer every night before I went to sleep. I gave thanks every morning for my father's healing. Ever since his youth, my father had wanted to touch his soul again. Now he was finding his grail, his male feelings, his love of the ocean. He moved to the ocean, stopped working, and rested.

Receptivity to the soul builds our immune systems. Creating a field of self-love and compassion around the body gives a strong boost to the immune system. It is time to slow down and walk in a sacred way again. We are at the end of a twenty-six-thousand-year cycle, and the intense light streaming to Earth now from the Central Sun is a massive radiation treatment of the cancer we have become to this planet. Let us not wait until we have cancer to send light and rejuvenation to our cells and explore our deep feelings.

The next medicine on this planet will involve frequency, vibration, the right use of light, and true dreaming in the dark. Let us love the dark, serpentine feminine, the Black Madonna. Let's "get down," as it is said in American black

culture. Let us find the dark womb of rebirth, the genius in
our darkness.

Black people understand the language of the soul. They
know the meaning of "soul food," "soul music," "soul language," and "soul brothers and sisters." Black people have
carried lighter-skinned people's projection of the shadow
long enough. The idea of "whites" and "blacks" creates conflict and separation. White people need to find the big black
gospel singer in their souls and let her sing. Black people
need to know how glorious they are in their nobility. As
members of the human family, we all need to learn how to
be humble in our souls and wildly creative.

We were told as children that we were bad and that some
people were evil. No one is bad or evil; this is a great human
illusion and an example of incorrect thinking. Badness is
a lie. Do not believe you are bad. You innately know what
is right or wrong for you. If it causes no harm to others,
you can act in any way that speeds the healing of your emotional body.

Science has tried to make machines of our bodies. It has
tried to make them clinical, splitting feeling from matter—
Materia, the Great Mother. Still, nature protects our deepest,
buried creativity. Nature values and loves human creativity.
Do not try to change the Earth; simply receive her.

We need to return to love. We need to love our bodies, for
we cannot get any denser. On this planet, we have sunk to
maximum density. Now the world is being hit by lightning,
and it is lightening up. We no longer need cancer to teach
us how to irradiate our bodies with love. Cancer asks us to
release systems of duty, work, reputation, and past relationships that do not serve our growth. It is a kind of houseclean-
ing. Likewise, heart attacks ask us to open our hearts. Let the

feelings of your heart be your prayer and mantra—not just
to God but to all beings.

Everything we endure has meaning and purpose. Matter
is loving. We are all loved. Some of us sought to go beyond
form to the stars and the infinite instead of allying ourselves
to our instincts of being held, touched, and appreciated. Yet
even in our rebellion, we have never left creation. Even while
seeking the heights and immortality, we find roots, depths,
and relatedness.

The way to truly heal cancer is through community.
Human beings naturally love community—communing
with nature. We can walk up a mountain and come down to
balance our brains. We can smoke the sacred pipe again and
greet the sun as it rises. Life is a great mystery, a rising dawn.
We must allow ourselves to be touched more. We often sleep
with our jaws and hands clenched. We need to relax and
support one another. We are all siblings on Earth, walking
through emotion, the gate of the moon, and mental clarity,
the gate of the sun. Let us become initiated and become who
we really are.

There is something beyond light that is more diverse
than our present reality. We are now being created in the
womb of the Earth. Cancer is congestion, a resistance to
rebirth. Let yourself feel the humming of the great preg-
nancy and nurture yourself through it.

We all have unique talents and gifts. Community is how
we fit together in a web. Our integrity and love build a community from within to support us, signaling the end of isolation. Relationships are a great mystery. Ask for them and
learn. To accept our differences and still be joined is the paradox of marriage. Discover the mystery of joining in order to
become more individualized.

Cancer is the call to love matter, to consciously partake in the birth of our species. We are divine children being born with a planetary body. Together we are opening to a new world of color, sound, and pure feeling. We have reached the end of our ego development as a species and are now preparing to meet our Creator, both inside and out. This is our second childhood. The time to play a new role in a community is now. Our karma is over. An infusion of electricity is pouring into us for integration. Let us open like the membranes around the Earth.

The boundaries of the Earth's womb are expanding wide to take in everything—all our experiences of incarnation and creation. The fields surrounding our bodies are expanding and becoming transparent.

Let go of any restrictive hesitation, and find the seed ideas and feelings associated with every experience. Talk to creation. Learn to read the stars. Walk outside to become more aware. The sky bends down to you, asking you to read it and feel protected under its sheer expanse of blue. You are vast. School is ending here. Between the years 1992 and 2013, the amount of light streaming to Earth will be accelerating exponentially. Your life is quickening.

If cancer is a congestion, a resistance to the light, then eat your shadow. Digest your past and convert it into raw life force. Express and eat the anger in your liver, and express it creatively. This conversion of the past into electricity in the body can rejuvenate you now.

Congestion is simply unfeeling fear. Do not respond to it; just witness it. Take a stand in life. Say no. Neither give in nor fight. Be a warrior, attached neither to winning nor to losing. Fear is not who you are. Fear can tell you when some-

thing is amiss. Just witness it without giving it much attention. It will eventually grow tired and leave.

Healing is an act of grace. It is returning to creation, to
the way things inherently are. Life tells a flower to bloom and
a bird to migrate, and it also teaches us how to be human and
curious. Create the desire to be healed. Be cured in order to
become a healer.

Healing is a call to build a soul container. If you have
soul, you can be penetrated by light and life. Too much light
and not enough container is the cause of many people's
deaths. To create a container to receive the light, make pottery, weave, draw, do something artistic. Art is the creation of
a soul vessel for the penetration of Spirit. Build a new womb
in your dreams. Create a grail for our times. That is the call
of cancer. Make a soul to receive your healing. Or if you
must die, write a new myth for those who are still living.

As I realized emotionally all that I have shared in these
pages, my father's cancer left his body. He healed himself and
gave me the gift of his understanding. My father leaned on
me, physically resting on my shoulder for a long, long time.
He was silently telling me, "You are the strong one now." He
passed on to me something masculine that I had been waiting for all my life.

I felt my father's acknowledgment of my soul. A beauty
grew in his eyes as he accepted his children and their role in
his life. His vulnerability made him seem stronger in my
eyes. The old Taurus bull finally let us go.

THE RAM

*I*f my father had been a bull for most of his life, I had been a ram. My father's cancer helped him transform his bull nature, and it also helped me look more deeply into my own negative masculinity. Unknowingly, I had made the archetypal Ram, the shadow side of myself, into an enemy. Now I had to look it in the eye and make it my ally.

Damien had taught me about the shadow side of my father. The Ram is an initiator, a Mars/Aries warrior who is fixated on logos, knowledge, competition, and the control of nature. But while the Ram can lead to a fixation on power and the loss of love, it is also the wise solar sheep that is so well loved in India.

Once, a woman came to me for a session and told me the following story. She had driven to Truchas, a small town north of Santa Fe. She walked out of her car near a hill and began climbing, picking wildflowers. A ram spotted her and charged full-speed in her direction. She was too far from her car to make it back in time.

Seeing the ram charging, the woman immediately calmed herself by breathing deeply. She felt she could face

125

the ram and even let go of life if she had to. The ram came on full force, but she stood her ground. Then, just before the animal smashed into her, it suddenly lowered its head and dug its horns into the Earth only inches from her toes.

That woman had made peace with her ram nature. Many women have not been so fortunate. In the Greek myth of Phrixos and Helle, a ram saves a boy and girl from a persecuting stepmother who wants to kill them. They learn of the plot and escape on the back of a ram, flying into the sky. The girl, Helle, looks down and falls into the sea and drowns, while the boy is safely set down in a new kingdom. Safe from his stepmother, Phrixos sacrifices the ram and hangs its fleece from a tree. Later Jason and the Argonauts go in search of the ram's fleece.

The Ram represents naive, unreflective, masculine intensity. Helle and most women suffer around Ram energy. A Ram man cannot listen to what his female side is telling him.

In the myth of Psyche and Eros, one of Psyche's tasks is to gather the fleece of rams. She learns to collect the hair from the bushes and not to bother the actual beasts, thereby avoiding a bloody confrontation. When an archetype takes over the unconscious, it can be dangerous; however, if, like Psyche, we can have a relationship with the Ram without allowing it to possess us, we can mine its rich wisdom and energy. And when we sacrifice the Ram, we give up our inflated identification with power—guns, missiles, war, control of feeling and the feminine—and convert its energy into creative potential.

Mars contains the word *ram*. To mar is to damage or deface. When the word *ram* is in someone's name, it means they have participated in some form of abuse of power in this or in past lives. In Babylonian and Sumerian myth, there is a character called Marduk, the usurper, the son of Enki. Until he is finally humbled, he is a destroyer.

Mars, the name of the mythical Roman god of war and, I believe, a former warrior planet, is the root of the term *martial arts*. According to intuitive information I have received, even our moon was once used as a military base during ancient star wars. Many people on Earth are descendants of refugees from these past wars and conflicts. Inhabitants of planets in the constellation Orion once waged a galactic war against the Pleiades and other star systems. These wars are over, and peace has returned to all other worlds except Earth. We have been quarantined here, cut off from communication with our own and other galaxies for some time.

Here on Earth, the northern Aryans destroyed the Dravidian culture of southern India. Warrior clans invaded and pillaged the south for gold and land, creating a pattern of enslavement. Extraterrestrials such as the Nibiruans did the same, enslaving human beings for minerals, access to Earth knowledge, and control of the planet. The Atlanteans created half-animal, half-human servants to do their menial work.

Myths of the Ram and the Rama empire in India are detailed in the wars described in the *Ramayana* and the *Mahabharata*. The past age of Aries on this planet gave rise to the Atlantean patriarchy and eventually to the Roman Empire, the pinnacle of patriarchy in the last five-thousand-year cycle. Roman, too, contains the word *ram*.

Some years ago, I did healing sessions with a series of children whose grandparents had been high-ranking Nazi officials. They all had *ram* in their names. While working with them, I started to dream of my last life. I was a fifteen-year-old Jewish girl in Dachau. I had a group of girlfriends in the camp, and we made jokes about the Nazis. Even as people around us were being gassed and tortured, I would tell everyone, "There is no such thing as death." I showed no fear around the Nazis, and one day they beat me to death for my impudence.

In this life, I have met many of the girls from that same camp. We all share the same memories. Even my childhood nanny was a German woman who had fled the Nazis when she was fifteen years old. We had known each other before, and she found me in this life.

I could not forget what happened in Germany. All these people came to me to discuss the nature of their victim/ victimizer relationships. Had we victimized others before? Had we ourselves been inflated with power in earlier lives? The answer was often yes, and now was the time to clear it.

Many of these grandchildren of Nazis had huge shadows in their bloodlines that affected their thoughts. They were fighting high priests, rams, and minotaurs in their dreams. In treating them, I saw that the Nazis could have used their knowledge of spirit for good but chose mass control instead. These grandchildren had psychic gifts and needed to purify their bloodlines in order to use them wisely.

With the advent of the Age of Aquarius, the cycle of war on this planet was ending, and people came to me in droves to heal their wounded male warriors. I saw in people's psyches how alcohol and "ramming" were often related. People who strongly felt the influence of their fathers were distant, aloof, unemotional, or mentally and emotionally abusive. Often they created fantasy images of magicians or altruistic fathers in order to compensate. Some even created an inner male magician who would save them when they drank or deliver them from car accidents when they were on drugs. Others were enslaved by child fantasy figures who had become internal elementals with wills of their own. Part of my work was to release clients from high priests and male teachers who had used or abused women and boys. Five thousand years of male abuse patterns were finally clearing.

When I was a child, I was naturally left-handed. Beginning in kindergarten, my schoolteachers made sure I used only my right hand. Patriarchal values stress one side of the brain over the other. I was taught to be rational and intellectual from a very young age. As an adult, I began to redevelop my left-handedness, consciously valuing creativity and the feminine and healing my betrayal. This is only one subtle example of an abusive pattern in our culture.

The children I treated who had Ram mothers often complained of having no boundaries that were honored. Their rooms had been invaded and their dreams psychically entered. These mothers had projected their own psyches onto their children. As a result, some of the children had abandoned their own souls at a very young age. Now, as women, they felt betrayed by patriarchal mothers. As men, they felt they had to caretake the sick mothers who sought to control their lives.

These Ram mothers were dominant, controlling, and narcissistic. Their children knew it, but needed help in order to bring their conflicts to a conscious resolution and release their devouring mothers from their psyches.

My work with the Ram energy brought me to a deeper understanding of the sacred marriage, the union of opposites. The name Mary also contains the word *ram*, but Mary was a positive Ram who initiated surrender. She transformed the Ram into healing and rebirth. She surrendered her Ram to a higher power and was impregnated by that power. She sacrificed the Ram in her psyche and surrendered to Eros, the spirit of love. The Ram brings trauma, drama, and the clash of armies, but it also holds the potential marriage of opposites.

The myth of Osiris and Seth and the lifting of the fourteen veils of self is crucial for understanding the inner marriage. In this story, Osiris is a divine king who has ruled Egypt for twenty-eight years. He is also a great musician and artist, the life principle associated with Eros, and his role is to teach men and women about the balance of the creative and destructive elements in the human psyche.

Seth, or *set*, is the root word for "separation." He represents the evil one, the outcast who is shunned by society. He is the one who is always told he is bad, dark, wrong, a sociopath. Seth believes that Osiris has become inflated with his own power and must be sacrificed to the feminine, so he murders him at the end of a great lunar cycle, the cycle of the feminine.

In order to kill Osiris, Seth takes the form of a wild boar. Thus, Osiris, the sun god, is destroyed by a dark, bullish masculinity. Seth is the shadow in every male, betraying his brother through destructive jealousy. Osiris, on the other hand, is a king, a solar hero whose sacrificial blood will refertilize the Earth. Together, these two form a creative duality, an expression of the war that goes on within all of us.

This myth tells us that the enemy is not outside but within. We have only separated ourselves from him. We need to give up the Ring of Power taken from the Earth in previous incarnations and give it back to the land. This is our conscious duty and also the deep truth that inspired J.R.R. Tolkien's trilogy, *The Lord of the Rings*.

To continue with our myth, Isis is the wife and queen of Osiris. She represents the sister, lover, and mother—our conscious feminine side. Weeping for her dead lover, she assumes the form of a hawk and flies over his corpse. This is what we do, too. Many women and men dream of their male side as dead, numb, unfeeling, and severely wounded and confined. It is the female side that watches these scenes of inner death. Isis finds Osiris's body floating down the Nile and puts it in a tree—a symbol of blood lineage—for safekeeping.

Patriarchal bloodlines began in Egyptian culture. Today, last names are handed down from the father's side of the family. Even the Bible was rewritten to exclude Rachel, Leah, Sarah, and the other female leaders of the twelve tribes. Israel was originally a matriarchal culture. The patriarchy has rewritten history as *"his* story"—a story of war and conquest—and almost universal amnesia has set in over time. Thus, in the patriarchal version of history, Eve is portrayed as a temptress, the root of all evil, when she and the serpent are actually helping humanity to discover wisdom.

With the help of Thoth, the Egyptian god of wisdom and a positive male teacher, Isis releases Osiris from the Tree of Life. She frees him from his earthbound incarnations. Later, Seth finds the body of Osiris, cuts it into fourteen pieces, and scatters it over the landscape.

Like the body of Osiris, we are all fragmented in our male sides. We are dismembered, rent, torn apart. When we try to penetrate another without the balance and wisdom of the soul, we tear ourselves apart through rape, greed, control, and ego sexuality, separating ourselves even further from those we hurt. But the wounds we inflict on others are also

inflicted on ourselves, and we lose a part of our psyche in
the process.

However, there is great hope in dismemberment.
According to another Greek myth, the goddess Artemis,
a virgin huntress, goes bathing in a forest stream. A curious
youth named Actaeon sees her. When he looks at the goddess, she turns him into a stag, and he is torn to pieces by his
own dogs, manifestations of his own underworld. Artemis
loves stags, and thus Actaeon becomes the very thing she
loves. In his dismemberment, he represents the sacrifice of
the youthful lover-god of the goddess.

In the Osiris story, with the aid of Thoth once again, Isis
finds thirteen parts of Osiris, her missing male side, and puts
them magically back together as one. The soul, the anima of
a man and the female side of a woman, can do this. However,
the fourteenth part of Osiris, his penis, Isis cannot find
because she does not have one herself. So she creates a new
one out of wood, and with a little of his sperm, she impregnates herself. She surrenders in that moment to God, becoming the feminine one-in-herself. Later, she gives birth to a
divine child named Horus, a falcon.

After discerning what parts of himself have been severed,
a male transforms his inner Ram—his negative, thrusting
self-will—into resurrection, creativity, art, and Earth stew-
ardship. He does this with the help of any wise elder, mentor, or teacher working in conjunction with his anima, or
female side. Dreams are helpful in discerning what parts have
been severed. The process from erection and phallic will to
resurrection and sacrifice of the Ram can be accomplished
through work as varied as dreams and martial arts. Men are
learning the mysteries of the grail again and becoming
embodiments of Osiris.

As the story continues, Horus, the new personality who represents enlightened self-will and the positive animus of a man or woman, goes to battle with Seth to avenge his father. Meanwhile, Osiris is in a coma in the underworld. His son lives in the upper world, and the two must now come together. Horus defeats Seth in the end, and father and son become one in the birth of a new aeon.

As the Horus archetype incarnates en masse in coming generations, grounded star children will learn how to face Seth and the Ram without feeling any separation. My prayer is that they will be birthed and raised with great love, nurtured by both parents and by multigenerational communities. This is only now beginning, and we have the privilege of helping it along. Our inner work on these issues helps prepare the way, as in Native American tradition, for seven generations to come.

All myth speaks of separation, initiation, and return. We have all come to Earth in order to put the fourteen pieces of our inner male back together. How do we do this? First by acknowledging the gift of life, then by acknowledging our own self-worth.

Be happy you were born. The Mother, the Cosmic Egg sent out a message, an inner pull for you to come and impregnate her with your consciousness. You were wanted. You are enough. Return to your essence. You were a master before you came here. The Mother guards her sexuality, her womb, for your arrival. She is untainted by what people do on the surface. She is the membrane of your womb, protecting your life force, enveloping you in her loving arms.

Rams need not bear arms, but open their arms and hands with a balanced head, heart, and hand. The left hand receives, the right hand gives. Know there is a part of yourself that is always loved, no matter how you have lived in the past. The greatest security is knowing who you are and that you are loved.

How do we forget that we are loved unconditionally? Our physical mothers are often not the archetypal Mother. The word *sin* was the name of the moon goddess in Sumerian mythology. Eve is not evil; we would discover that the Garden of Eden is all around us if we could live in the moment. In our longing for paradise, we forget that it is right here and now.

Many of us blame the negative Mother, the Black Madonna, the Serpent Mother for our ills. In East Indian mythology, the Great Goddess Durga sends Kali, the Black Mother, to destroy the negative male demons who are ravaging the Earth through war. Kali emerges out of Durga's third eye and conquers the demons through the nondual perspective of the feminine. The Kala (masculine counterpart to Kali) in men is facing the negative shadow of patriarchal control. The fact that most tax money in America goes to the military is a clear indication of the Ram archetype in our society.

The Black Madonna is black because she is connected to her primal roots, the black obsidian in the center of the Earth. She is the woman who is rooted in her first chakra and who feels empowered to send her branches upward. She is an unknown part of the feminine psyche, emerging from the darkness. We men have made up numerous lies about women, which we disguise in language. The etymology of words is the path of Sophia, the goddess of wisdom. She can restore balance to language.

As our souls are born into the greater density of the Earth plane, we often forget who we are because of the shock of the birth entry. The pineal gland becomes disconnected. Children who are born underwater or with dolphins present do not experience this disconnection. They come into life more alert and knowing.

I have swum with dolphins many times and witnessed the underwater births of their babies. This experience has helped to heal my own birth trauma. The dolphins taught me to play in the womb again and encouraged me to live in a community that honors sacred birthing practices. A dolphin pod—which is really an extended family—includes up to ten generations of dolphins. We, too, need the wisdom and companionship of communities that are multigenerational.

Density is merely a shift from one state of matter to another. The light is still inside you, and it must be felt, realized, and shared in order for you to benefit from it. You developed a body, along with all its density and weight, in order to learn how to create—to have an adventure in time. You had to release your sky notion of immortality in order to participate in life and not rush existence.

Savor life. Build for ecstasy. Do only what you love to do. You came here to be fully realized as a creator god, through self-love. Right action and feeling in the present frees you from past pain and suffering. You were brought to the level of greatest density on this planet for the sake of your ego development, bodily strength, and individuality, and you can go no further into density at this time. *This is when the hummingbirds come.*

When your identity is formed, you can let go into the emerging unknown self. You become impregnated with new instructions, the next phase of evolution and mutation. The process of identity reverses itself, moving back to original essence and will. After differentiation of your male and

female, you are ready for union. Separation, dismemberment—the rip in the world—creates the call to be initiated,
a return to the self. When density reaches its outermost
limit, it is transformed into enlightenment.

In looking back over the myth of Osiris, it is interesting
to note that Isis is impregnated when she surrenders. In
giving up her ego to the greater self, she conceives a new
animus, a new son, a new personality. In the future, women
will once again teach men the mysteries of sexuality and intimacy. We must ask for partnerships in which "two solitudes
protect and border and greet each other," as Rilke says.

We men, too, must be impregnated. We can surrender
our female sides and become receptive to impregnation by
the divine sun. The grail is a cauldron of the soul that is penetrated and filled with God. The Native Americans participate in Sundances in which men are wounded, symbolically
dismembered, in order to embody the full energy of the sun.
This is a ritual action, a sacrifice for the good of the entire
tribe. When the Ram bows to the woman in Truchas and a
man gives up naked power plays and asks for an equal partnership with the feminine, there is a sacred marriage of
mutual surrender. The marriage becomes the vessel for the
"third force," the penetration of the higher self.

We are attracted to another person because of the frequency of that person's soul. Sometimes, this can be an
infatuation for which we are not emotionally prepared.
We animate each other. We project our male and female
sides onto one another, and the personalities of our inner
male and female often mirror those of our parents.

In most relationships, there is a moment of stasis or first
bliss that leads inevitably to separation. We then disengage

our projections to see the person in front of us as they really are. At that moment, we often see the shadow—and afterward go through a dark time projecting our negativity onto our partners. It is difficult to own our shadows, but relationships give us an opportunity to project them onto another and then integrate them into ourselves, eventually releasing the projection from our mates.

As we own our shadows, we go through the dark night of the soul to its very limit. At that point, the darkness transforms into light and creates a mental union, a marriage of the head, that leads to initial bliss and contentment. This is where most people stay. The next stage is one in which both partners clear and detoxify their bodies for a full somatic union, a *hieros gamos,* or holy marriage. Then all the grief, denial, and unloved parts of ourselves become transformed.

After that, our consciousness shifts to the lower body, our source of inner heat and creation. We surrender our bodies to be filled, impregnated. As all the chakras clear through great fire and emotion, there is a mystical union of opposites, an orgasm, a humming.

In this we reenact the drama of the Earth. The cosmic egg is opened to receive the rainbow, to complete its covenant with the stars. Our inner being resonates with the center of the planet, which in turn resonates with the center of the galaxy, the Central Sun. We build a triangular vessel composed of the male, the female, and the divine child.

The cup made by the Holy Spirit, the vessel of Sophia, is the feminine symbol in men and women that receives the divine. Men are creating new *male* cups as the gap in feeling is bridged. The God in us is the unconscious wanting to be heard, seen, penetrated. The cup is shaped like an open egg. As the soul cup opens within, it is completed by the sun spirit without, and their union is a joyful rapture.

Spirit is the lance. In the Arthurian legends, Lancelot impregnates and honors the mystery of the female. A woman who teaches tantra can help a man withhold his semen and learn the deeper mysteries of sexuality. Men can learn this procedure in order to bring the energy of sexuality up into the heart for a truly cosmic orgasm. The dance of opposites is a mating dance in which the goal is conscious union with the Divine. The whole Earth participates in this sacrament.

Priests need to get married and explore the mysteries of creation. Sexuality is a holy act. The feminine does not have to be idealized in order to create a deeper partnership. The feminine wants real human love. Even when there are no more secrets, the mystery of love grows stronger.

During a rebirthing session, I discovered that when I was in my mother's womb I was a twin. For four months, my twin sister developed next to me. Her soul then entered my body, and I experienced the union of Isis and Osiris in the womb state. After four months, she was stable enough to bring me a sense of wholeness. After that time, she developed psychically inside of me rather than physically in the womb. I remembered this during the time of my own dreams of the sacred marriage.

As my ego developed and I could sufficiently differentiate the male and female within, I dreamed of an inner marriage and experienced a full-body orgasm. It took four years for this process to fully manifest in dreamwork, and it consumed my life during that time. But that inner work led to the deep teaching and counseling of others in later years. It also became the foundation for the insights of this book.

CHRIST AND
THE PUER AETERNUS

*T*he Earth has its own schedules; humans can neither speed up nor slow down the natural unfoldment on this planet. At one time, extraterrestrials wanted to hasten evolution here and caused the destruction of Atlantis. According to myth, they gave the Atlanteans advanced technology, and in their desire to dominate the Earth, the Atlanteans misused it. Ten thousand years ago, they activated a great crystal, causing an electromagnetic cataclysm. This abuse of Earth's natural resources is a symbolic warning for our present age.

The Puer Aeternus, the masculine archetype of eternal youth in our psyches, also wants to speed up life and hurry events along. The Nazis are a prime example of a people who became obsessed by the *puer* archetype. Overidentification with the Puer Aeternus can create an idealistic need to change the Earth.

We humans do not change the larger cycles of evolution on Earth. We must learn humility and relatedness to the web of life. God is an Earth concept. We are here to bring our souls into our bodies and then bring the God self inside us, incarnated on Earth.

Indigenous people accept life as it is. They listen to the wind, the songs, and the cycles of nature. They divine and interpret what they perceive on a deep level. Nothing on this planet can be taken literally. It is all metaphor, a great play. When we stop just surviving and begin to live in grace, we can discover and appreciate the discipline of listening to the wind and the cycles humming through the Earth.

In facing my own puer nature, I had to risk closing the gap between childhood and adulthood, feeling and thinking. My star self had to accept death, deep feelings, and even the breaking of my own heart. I found it difficult to be in my body, but I had to learn about the mundane as well as the divine. Marriage is both banal and a great mystery. I had always felt isolated and ahead of my time. I had to learn how to be in the here and now, how to make a living—how to be ordinary.

When I first opened spiritually, all I thought of was light. However, I have learned that too much fixation on the light creates a huge shadow. The myth of Lucifer, the light-bringer, is the story of an angel who wanted only to serve God and not human beings. He was cast down to be humbled on Earth. We often feel cast down, descending into the prison of *maya*, illusion. The shadow of the light is an unfeeling coldness in the heart. If we want only to be in the sky realms serving spirit, we become flighty, detached, unemotional, and uncommitted. Our task as humans is to bring feeling to the coldest, darkest places in our bodies, to redeem our tainted image of ourselves.

In the myth of Osiris, there comes a time for Seth to be freed. He is the other divine twin, as in the stories of Cain tand Abel, Judas and Christ. He is the destroyer. We need to free Seth and forgive him, transform the rebel without a cause into an Earth steward and a partner of the feminine. We need to develop the ability to act both as sensitive men and as warriors at appropriate times.

Seth serves the Goddess and redeems himself by slaying the serpent Apophis every night. He cooperates with the sun god and integrates his aggression. Seth and the Goddess always foster individuation and transformation. Seth masters the rainbow serpent, the kundalini energy. The slayer and the slain become one. This is a high order of self-sacrifice.

Shamans are similarly initiated by being dismembered or devoured by animals such as jaguars, tigers, whales, or bears. They make a pact with nature to be consumed by spirit and then to heal and embrace all life—both the high and the low, the dark and the light. Life comes from life. When we face the dark lord in ourselves, we can redeem our Sethian shadows and make them our allies.

I believe that some of the early colonizers of Earth had animal forms, such as the Lizard People. These people show up in hundreds of my clients' dreams, often with remarkable similarities; perhaps they are symbolic of the reptilian brain. These reptilian people never knew how to feel. They were immortal. They did not understand death and thought of humans as inferior. They controlled the Earth, focusing on mining colonies in such places as South Africa, Iraq, and Peru. They mined outer gold, forgetting the gold inside.

Many of these Reptile People have reincarnated on Earth at this time. They have come back to learn about emotional responsibility and be freed from the past. Now is the time of their baptism, the immersion of their diamond bodies into the center of the Earth.

In the summer of 1991, many of my clients were dreaming about Reptile People. I heard about sightings of these beings all over the world. One day, I met a group of American soldiers and asked one where they were going. He told me point blank, "You'll think I'm nuts, but we're going to fight Lizard People in the Nevada desert. These creatures look like reptiles, but they walk on two legs." I told this soldier of my clients' dreams and the synchronicity of meeting him.

Even while I was writing this book in 1992, a friend of mine who works in a gem store told me the following story. "These military men came into the store and wanted to buy crystals to protect themselves," she said. "I asked them why. They told me they were going to fight Lizard People in the desert." She then told me her dreams of these people, which were very positive. There is much more occurring on Earth than we imagine.

Eventually, I realized that the key to healing the puer in myself lay in adolescent forms of spirituality. I had to bond with my father and initiate a break from my mother. I had to create my own rite of passage into manhood. I had to find Eros, feeling, relatedness. I had to own the shadow of the past.

The Lizard People are now seeing clear reflections of their past control in the military. Perhaps the soldier I struck up a conversation with was going through a rite of passage of his own, facing his darkest fear in the image of a reptilian person. For myself, I had to leave the paradise of childhood and find an earthy spirituality that was connected to instinct. I also needed the counsel of an older person I could trust. As a puer, I had fallen in love with the shadow of my father. I had become a bisexual man looking for my father's love.

For years, I dreamt of my father as either aloof or inces-
tuous. Then one night, I had a breakthrough. I had been
working consciously to bring feeling to the gap between my
father and myself as a child. I dreamt that my father offered
me food—an apple, a symbol both of consciousness and of
the Fall—and I took his nourishment. In later dreams, he
held me, played sports with me, and asked for intimacy
again. He became a nurturer.

My inner father had returned. He incarnated as a loving
man inside my soul, and that changed how I saw the world.
Without even looking at people's bodies, I fell in love with
their souls. I began to have loving male friends who were not
afraid to touch or reach out. I began to find men who shared
male feelings. I also met other men who were reuniting lost
parts of themselves.

Men who love men are like positive charges building
a fire. Women who love women are like negative charges
drawing in energy. Men burn energy, and women gather it.
When I was younger, I wanted the heat, the intensity of the
fire. Then, sex was a pseudo-religious experience of ecstasy,
not a true meeting of souls. As I grow older, I find that I
want intimacy rather than intensity. I feel like the Sufi poet
Rumi, seeing God in the blacksmith.

Gay people need to experience the inner marriage of
their male and female sides and seek intimacy before ego
sexuality. If your sexuality stems from parental abuse, then
begin the process of dreaming about that parent nurturing
you, feeding you. Ask for a transformation in the Dreamtime
of your inner world. This can profoundly affect your outer
relationships.

Homosexuality can become a path toward the inner
union of male and female, serving as a sort of stage on which

to develop deeper feelings. In ancient times, following the
ice ages, gay people served as tribal bards and healers. They
traveled from town to town in theatrical troupes, singing,
dancing, dispensing remedies, and performing healings.
Many men and women in such towns would leave their
families and join them if they felt called to do so.

In some traditional Native American cultures, gender
roles were more fluid than they are now. Gay men cross-
dressed and were initiated into both men's and women's
lodges. They were venerated as holy people and loved for
their outrageousness. Similarly, many lesbians were honored
by their tribes, took lovers, and became leaders. There are
also many stories of bisexuality among shamans. This sort
of tribal consciousness is building again in the world, and it
is promoting greater self-acceptance for all people.

"Gay," "bisexual," and "heterosexual" are all labels that
quickly dissolve when you see a person's innate humanity
and soul. Who are we to judge anyone? After all, many gay
souls today are healing past lives spent in homosexual priesthoods, secret societies, and warrior clans. Many gay men
today—men who were overtly masculine in past lives—are
just beginning to find their souls, often with great difficulty.
Loneliness and lack of community are big issues for everyone
in our society, but today we're undergoing both personal and
collective revolutions as members of a larger family.

Gay people have an affinity for aesthetics. They are often
too much like hummingbirds, though. In fixating on beauty,
they can lose track of the deeper roots of life. Life is imper-
fect, asymmetrical. Some artists—such as Navajo sand
painters—create objects with one aspect of the design or
construction just a little bit off in order to intentionally mirror the creation. Many people who have died of AIDS, which

most people perceive as an ugly disease, were deep apprecia-
tors of aesthetics.

It is time to really look at ugliness and not be so caught
up in the cult of beauty and the physical body. It is time for
a deeper initiation. The societal label of homosexuality as a
form of perversion—a kind of ugliness or evil—has done
great harm to life. Nothing is bad or evil. Let us find the
beauty in our shadows as a culture and explore our "ugly"
sides with the intention of healing them.

We all need to feel safe in order to open to our gifts as
human beings. There is great diversity in the psyche and in
sexuality. Sexuality actually includes a much wider spectrum
of orientations than most people realize. Many people—even
those who may not admit or practice it—are bisexual to
some degree. Androgyny is a result of diversifying our inner
male and female for eventual union. Many gay people have
lived recent lives as members of the opposite sex, and some
even come from androgynous worlds where sexuality is not
an issue. It is time for us to develop a more comprehensive
understanding and acceptance of diversity in sexuality, as
well as in the psychology of the soul.

Gay women often embody attributes of the Goddess.
They are often wise teachers and counselors, excellent herb-
alists, and positive witches. Gay men and Don Juan-type
males are often puers who are learning to break from a de-
pendency on their mothers in order to find genuine male
intimacy.

On the whole, men in our society carry deep mother
complexes. Mother's boys want to remain little boys forever
instead of adapting to the real world of relationships. After
thirty years, such men may still be relying on their parents
for support. They may dream they are great poets or vision-

aries or have fantasies of saving the Earth. They may embody the archetype of the Divine Son and become lovers of the Great Mother. They may be so identified with being a divine child or a winged god that they cannot face real hardship or difficulty and find their own place in the world. Or they may feel completely abandoned, endlessly searching for money and/or love.

My mother had a neurotic, frigid side, and I longed for warmth and love, often settling for money as a substitute. I knew her neurosis was really an inner cry for her to rise to a higher level. Her symptoms cried out to her individuality. She really was a healer, but she had to find her own empowerment as a woman. She needed to find the feminine as one-in-herself, the goddess Sophia.

For my own sake, I decided not to take care of my mother's emotional needs, but she constantly undermined my progress by slipping me money when my father wasn't looking. I finally said no. In order to find my own soul, I had to leave my mother's world.

That is the first essential thing: to leave our mother's world. Second, if we believe ourself to be too much of a divine youth, we must learn to integrate our shadow in order to become vital again. Working at a job that does not break our spirit provides a strength, independence, and entrepreneurship that is often stifled by our mother.

Third, we must embrace difficulty and conflict in order to find masculine courage. This also helps to develop leadership and bonding with other males. Conflict resolution is one of the great lessons of earthly life. Fourth, we men need to accept and embrace our ordinariness, just as medicine people are often humble and shy about their work.

Fifth, we need to see the difference between the woman

in our dreams, our anima figure, and our actual mother. The negative and positive sides of the feminine are different. They must be differentiated *within* in order for us to enjoy the warmth and nurturing of our inner woman.

Sixth, we need to create a stronger bond with our physical father. We need to find him and begin an ongoing conversation with him. And last, we need to find our own soul, our innermost self. We can do this by letting the Goddess be our guide to the inner Osiris.

Possessed by divine youth, a puer realizes that God is incarnating within him as the son of the Great Mother. This is how he becomes a true Osiris, his true self. Through the Great Mother, he confronts his Sethian shadow, is torn apart, and reemerges from the underworld with feelings and flexibility. The Goddess has been his guide to find the male Osiris, the beauty of a man who is finally one in himself.

Horus, the son of Osiris, lives beyond death and redeems his father. He is both an elder and a youth, both the archetypal "senex" and the puer. Dialogue between the old man and the youth within us is healing for the male psyche and connects us to Horus, our emerging male personality. Osiris is a horned god, the husband of the Mother Goddess. He finds the mother and the son and is resurrected to a new life through us. He teaches us about creativity, the value of the muse, and about the beauty of the underworld journey in which we find the discarded parts of our masculinity. He becomes modest, flexible, a world server. And ultimately, his destiny is fulfilled by taking care of the Earth, fertilizing the fields, and building community.

A puer is a man who is fixated on adolescent notions of spirituality and early sexual experiences. He does not adapt well to being in his body on Earth and wants to fly off without embracing love and discipline and contributing to community. In mythological terms, the puer appears as Horus bonding with his father in the underworld. He comes as a rainmaker to heal the wasteland, to bring his father soul knowledge.

In many ways, the puer is the visionary who is ahead of his time. If he can endure incarnation and fearlessly listen to his serpentine female depths and his male shadow, he can ultimately experience the sacred marriage, the union of earth and sky. In fact, today God is frequently incarnating on Earth—especially in Western culture—through this particular archetype, and that is why it is so important.

Let me tell you the story of one particular puer—myself—that will illustrate some of these points. When I was twelve years old, my older sister (who was twenty-six years old at the time) told me about giving her life to Christ and becoming born again, and she encouraged me to do the same. I had just become an individual with an ego, and I was being asked to surrender it to a higher power. This was the beginning of my medicine work.

I had a great deal of sexual shame as a child. At twelve, I had no one to talk to about things that deeply concerned me: masturbation, bisexuality, fetishes, and a burgeoning adolescent spirituality. I began to tell Christ everything, hoping he would heal me. I did not know how to integrate my fire.

My father wanted to teach me discipline, but I wanted to be nurtured. I had been severed from my mother when I was very young, and I transferred my feelings of love onto my father. His response was to distance himself. He was a workaholic. Even though he took me all over the world, I still felt that he favored my brother and that somehow I was not good enough for him. On the other hand, my father felt that I favored my mother. It was twenty-nine years before I developed a real intimacy with my dad. As a twelve-year-old, I gave up on my physical father and transferred all my needs to Christ. At least he and *his* father were one.

I was deeply sensual at seven and eight years old and developed a pronounced foot fetish. For years, I dreamed of feet—grounding myself through my feet, my soul entering through my feet, washing the disciples' feet, and so on. I became enamored of other people's feet, feeling that this was the most sensual part of the body. Feet became a wild obsession for me, an outlet for my sexual fantasies. I collected shoes and socks and even had an orgasm at age eight while dreaming about feet.

I began naturally to do the tantric technique of holding the point at the base of the penis that would block the passage of semen. Intuitively, I learned and practiced shooting sexual energy up my spine to my head. Even as a child, I felt the power of sexuality exploding through my body, and I intuitively experimented with tantric techniques. I kept all this a secret from my parents.

Then, as my sister "witnessed" to me about Christ, I felt this was the moment to heal my "sin" of fantasizing about sex. I wanted to shut down my feelings and have a personal relationship with Christ, a nonsexual animus figure. After she talked to me, I cried all night, releasing years of childhood guilt.

In this way, my sister initiated me into the Baptism of the Holy Spirit, a ceremony in which one asks for the Spirit to live inside and give words from the angels. I learned to empty all thoughts and sing to God in harmonic languages. The Pentecostals call this practice *glossolalia*. It is an ecstatic, private prayer-language to God. Often I would receive translations of the sounds I was making. This was a Gnostic principle from the doctrines of early Christian sects that I was familiar with from other lives, though my sister knew nothing of Gnosticism.

My conversion occurred during an era of charismatic masses, "Jesus People," and Pentecostalism. My parents vehemently opposed such practices. My father was a Catholic doctor who worked in a Catholic Hospital, and my mother was Greek Orthodox. I was allowed to read the Bible, but any other books that had religious overtones were taken away. For three years, I read the Bible, learning to decipher its pages on seven levels, as in the mystic Christian tradition. I would read beside a sewer stream behind my home. For hours, I would memorize the stories, letting the Holy Spirit guide me.

At fourteen years of age, I began to see Christ. This powerful being of love visited and talked to me about what I was reading and about how to live a full life. He told me we are all capable of being Christed beings and that Christ was an office, a title. I began to have dreams of Heliopolis in Egypt—where Christ is believed to have been initiated as a great master—of passing through the arched entryway there, and of a dove sitting on my shoulder after passing many initiations.

"Follow your heart," Christ told me. "Fundamentalism is full of dogmas and untruths. Learn to test the truth and let the Holy Spirit be your guide. You are being called to a fuller life. Listen to nature." That was his counsel.

Whenever Christ arrived, I used to see flames and letters above the foliage by the river. I also noticed that his heart was in the center of his chest, while mine was off to the side. I wanted to move my physical heart to the center of my body like Christ's. He became my constant guide and teacher.

Soon after these experiences, I started to lay hands on people. I went to see a faith healer, Katherine Kuhlman, and felt that I could do the same things she did. She called faith healing "being slain in the Spirit." In India they call it *shaktiput*. I started to practice *shaktiput* when I was fourteen. Then I met Sarah, a Japanese girl at school who was having experiences similar to mine. We began to hold prayer meetings. We would pray over people, read the Bible, and interpret it, creating a strong field of healing and intention.

Word began to spread about the amazing children who were having visions and channeling Spirit through their mouths and hands. Soon, scores of people were showing up to see us—even Buddhists, Hindus, and atheists. We went to charismatic Catholic masses, prayed with nuns and priests, and laid our hands on drug addicts to release their withdrawal symptoms. We listened to everyone's story and beliefs and never reacted from a closed heart.

Adolescent spirituality is often transcendent, vertical, ascensionist. It is very connected to the puer archetype, the Eternal Child. I was filled with wonder and innocence at that time, swept along by the masses of people in churches and prayer meetings and the depth of feeling in the songs.

I was also quite naive. As Robert Bly would say, I was showing my gold too soon. I went into churches and gave Bible lessons, relating my story of conversion. I laid hands on people in Catholic churches, converting many others through the Baptism of the Holy Spirit. At my provocation, my middle sister (twenty-six years old at the time), gave her life to Christ, too. Then came the backlash.

During this time, I heard some church people talk negatively about bisexuality, homosexuality, and women's rights

and how such things were a function of the devil. I wondered
why so many Christians were in the military. As I got to
know some Christians well, I began to see the hypocrisy of
their sermons against the backdrops of their everyday lives.
The call for money was relentless.

I also noticed that the pastors were not empowering people; they were *taking* power. I watched parishioners go to the
pastors for their advice and take it as God's truth. I watched
people give their power away constantly. God had power *over*
us, not *with* us, the pastors seemed to be saying.

Moreover, the human body was not treated as a temple; it
was considered something to be ashamed of. Human feelings
were abhorred and repressed. The Bible was taken literally,
losing its rich depth of meaning. When my older sister
talked with angels, her pastor said they were the fallen angels
of the devil, and she never listened for them again.

When I heard this, my heart sank. She took me to a store-
front church in Colorado Springs near where she lived at the
time when I was fourteen years old. The atmosphere was
intense. The minister was actually giving psychic readings
and doing *shaktiput*. Seven people prayed over my body, and
I experienced a huge emotional release. My sister called her
pastor to relay our excitement over the service, and he said
it was unclean, of the devil, and that we must purify ourselves quickly.

I gave up on my sister. She had once been physically
beautiful, sensual, and hilariously willful. But she had been
born without kneecaps and had little flexibility. She always
feared falling on her knees. She was a feisty Aquarian, a col-
lege debater who eventually married a man in the military.
When her marriage was falling apart, she gave herself to
Christ, and miracles happened—her marriage was strength-

ened, and she felt new meaning in her life. However, I missed the sensual, debating sister with a quick mind.

Now she preached without flexibility. She had learned to be on her knees before Christ and her pastor. She had surrendered to both of them. I felt her beauty, her loneliness, and her desire to really connect with people emotionally. I watched her scream at her husband and children. Maybe there was hope in those outbursts.

Preachers talked of hellfire and brimstone. I couldn't tell anyone in the church about my talks with Christ by the river. Christ was telling me to be human, to go back into the world and see the sacred in the mundane. "You do not need another religion. This is the time of your return to grace," he had said.

I dreamt of the Pleiades and the diamond body created through the stars inside Christ's body; I realized what humanity could become. I saw that Christ was my mentor, my master teacher. Every puer needs a senex, an older, wiser man to balance his adolescent spirituality. Christ gave me lessons on being in my body and embracing my sexuality. He was just the elder I needed.

Years later, I would read *A Course in Miracles* and heal my Christian past, releasing all institutionalized religions. I had always felt that societies and institutions were too dependent on central authority. When this central authority collapsed, the civilization, church, or institution would inevitably fall. I knew deep inside that the soul lived on in culture, art, and the beauty of creation. I began to study art again, painting aspects of the feminine for six years, meeting the Goddess, returning to nature, drawing plants and birds.

At Bible meetings, I saw a call to innocence that masked a darker presence. By yearning for transcendence while not

owning their devilish shadows, many of these people had
denied their fundamental humanness. It was an example of
how the fascination with Spirit can tyrannize form. These
people seemed to have no acceptance of diversity when it
came to biblical ideals. (Even the ecstasy of this particular
religion seemed reptilian—full of visions that separated one
from heaven on Earth.)

The New Age people, I noticed, were just as messianic,
relying on ascension and spaceships to fulfill their dreams.
I remembered being airlifted in other lives during cataclysms, but I always returned to Earth to learn the lessons
of the soul—the lessons of joy that are learned only by
descending into a body.

I wanted to learn of the ashes, the darkness that creates
gold. I wanted to take in all life and learn about bodily
awareness by jumping into cold streams and waking up with
aliveness. I learned to love the sensual pagan in me and to see
everything as sacred. My body was the Earth and the stars;
we were one cosmic egg. Gradually, through discerning all
my inner voices, I met and came to know intimately the
many archetypes of my polytheistic soul. I learned never
to listen to only one voice.

My other sister—the one I had converted—eventually
became allergic to everything, including chemicals, most
foods, and even the sun. She had to live in a sealed bubble in
Texas for a while in order to be tested for allergies. She had
separated herself from the feminine Earth, the sensual. She
married a wonderful man who was paralyzed from the waist
down. She led a life of solitude, suffering gently. I told Christ
that I would not live a life addicted to suffering. According
to my belief in the symbology of the number *twelve*, there

were twelve paths to godhood, and only three required
suffering. What about the other nine?

A big part of the problem, it seemed to me, was that the
great Mother Earth, the Goddess, had not been taken into
the church. The church did not recognize matter, so it developed materially, becoming a paternal institution—both
literal and fundamentalist. The aloof God of this church
eventually incarnated as a man. Divinity was seen as masculine, not feminine. Most of us—both men and women—
still need to incarnate the feminine God in us. Sophia is here
to help us do this.

Christians who are overidentified with logos, or higher
knowing, often lose their feeling side to the unconscious.
The soul must be allowed to return from below. Logos has
emphasized spiritual victories over the sensual. The more
rules the church made, the more humans separated themselves from their anima. Thus, the Goddess fell and was
relegated to the lowest levels in our myths. Over the years,
I rediscovered my anima, not as the Virgin Mary but as
the chthonic Mary Magdalene.

I would like to share a different story about Christ from
the one taught by the church. This is my story—the story of
Christ that I believe has been stolen from us by the church.

Mary, the mother of Jesus, or Mari Anatha, was the holy
priestess of a temple in Egypt. She studied with the Essenes
but was a master in her own right. She went through a sacred
marriage ritual with the horned god. She was impregnated
by a representative of God on Earth, a man who became a
divine king. He would be sacrificed to play this role in the
divine marriage.

Then Christ came to end the physical sacrifice of the horned god. Christ was born to Mary as a twin, and his twin brother was Judas. Here we have the divine pair—Seth and Osiris, Cain and Abel, the dark and light—together.

Mary Magdalene became the new high priestess of the Egyptian temple when she was quite young. She prepared for her bridegroom, Jesus Christ. When the time came, she descended into the underworld and purified her soul, as a priestess would know how to do. She learned about the mysteries of resurrection. This is why she later was the first to see Christ at the tomb after he rose.

Mary Magdalene, this representative of the Goddess on Earth, was married to Christ. Their union was both holy and sexual, and their marriage produced a daughter.

Judas was the former lover of Mary Magdalene, hence Mary's reputation as a harlot. Yet it was Judas who played Christ's betrayer and who later redeemed himself by becoming the new Christ child's caretaker. After Christ was resurrected, he instructed Judas to care for Mary Magdalene and his child as a surrogate father. Thus, Mary Magdalene, the Black Madonna archetype, married the dark male betrayer, while Mari Anatha and Christ, the great princess and prince, were resurrected as ascended masters.

Mary Magdalene and Judas lived on, dedicated to rejuvenating the Earth through the spirit of Christ's child, a female Horus figure. They visited Alexandria, Lourdes, Fatima, Glastonbury, Iona, and other holy spots around the world, and churches were built in their memory.

Mary Magdalene was visiting the places of the Goddess to find a home for her child, the seed of Christ in humankind. Thus, she was an earthy goddess, redeeming the shadow of matter. Judas, in turn, redeemed the Dark Brother, becoming a father, an Earth steward, and a homemaker for Christ on Earth.

This story is based on a balanced foursome. Christ and Mari Anatha, the great Puer Aeternus and his mother, live on in the spirit world after their resurrection. Meanwhile, Mary Magdalene, the Black Madonna, and her consort, the chthonic male, Judas, remain on Earth as teachers. The earthly masculine and feminine become responsible for the care and nurturing of the divine child in matter. Hence, positive and negative, animus and anima, become balanced: we all inherit the divine child and embrace our parental shadows.

I enjoy this story. In it, the Judas, the dark woodsman in me, is loved and taught the value of service. Similarly, Mary Magdalene, the gypsy woman and temple prostitute in me, is redeemed. This couple remains on Earth, inside us all, while our other Christed selves live on in the upper worlds. As above, so below. The church has robbed us of this story. It is the deeper chthonic mystery of the joining of upper and lower worlds within us: how our instincts can nurture the Christ child in the sacred marriage of our bodies.

Eventually, the puer in me began to seek older men as teachers. I lived in nature, climbed trees, and reawakened my instincts. I wanted to know my human father; instead, I found art teachers and mentors who helped me find my muse, my anima.

At Georgetown University, I began to produce elaborate works of art that I called "Catherine Rooms." The work, which eventually occupied a total of three rooms in the university gallery, was based on Saint Catherine of Alexandria, a woman of scholarly wisdom who was versed in the arts,

sciences, and poetry of the twelfth century. She became my
muse and inspiration when I was twenty years old.

The church fathers, jealous of Catherine's knowledge,
had crucified her on a wheel. I created large-scale exhibits of
her symbolic life. The exhibits began with the death of the
feminine: a woman lying in her grave, with films of urban
destruction projected on the walls. In this first room, the
Goddess appeared as Lilith, destroyer of cities.

Adjoining rooms were filled with paintings of cardinals,
popes, patriarchs, and colonialists who had judged Catherine
and lost their muses. A few ascetics stood in the corners of
these rooms, symbolically trying to keep Catherine's faith
alive. Other rooms contained images of the world turning
upside down: earthquakes, tables on the ceilings, empty pic-
ture frames, bank collapses, handwritten letters of abuse, and
abandoned children. I even included broken machines with
the word *entropy* written on them.

At the end of the last room were blank canvases, films
of nature, women as part of the landscape, and a female figure
in the Earth depicted with a paintbrush in her hand. A man
painted in the corner was emerging from the woods to greet
me, and then came a giant ocean wave and a series of spheres
intended to portray the connection of the soul to the self.

At the end of this maze was the sun, a mandala of yellow
and gold, the circle of completion. I had found my muse, my
anima, and together we met the man in the wood emerging.
This was the beginning of healing my soul through a kind of
prophetic art.

Saint Catherine broke the wheel of karma to which the
church had chained her. They crucified her on that wheel
according to her legend, but she broke it. When agents of the
church pierced her side, milk came out, just as milk was said

to pour from the tomb of Osiris. Osiris was the resurrected man in me, while Catherine was the resurrected woman, the feminine Christ figure. She could never die, for she represented my soul.

I met my anima for years in dreams after that. Gradually, she became less idealized, more like my partner. That is when I met my spirit wife.

PART THREE

HUMMINGBIRD
MEDICINE

SPIRIT WIFE

I met my spirit wife by the railroad tracks in Santa Fe. She was waiting for me, like a train, to take me on a mysterious journey. No one could see her but me.

"Are you my muse, my anima, a part of me?" I asked her.

"All of the above," she said. "I am your twin fully grown. I come in the form of a Native American woman because that is the path I have followed. I am not attached to that path; we must go beyond all paths. You are a part of my soul that is my husband, and I came to find you when you were open to receive me."

I looked at her. She was my other whole self wanting to blend. She was my soul returning to me as my wife. She said we had three sons and one daughter. "I knew you in another lifestream, but in this one we are already married," she said. "I hold the dreams of our future."

"What is our future?" I asked.

"To work together to help you become whole as a man, as my husband. To help you learn to be a leader in community. I am your beloved, and I have a form that you can see. This is a mystery. I am one of the fulfillments of your dream."

I loved this strange, ethereal woman. She would come over and find me in restaurants, in beds. I felt secure, comforted by her enduring presence in my life. She said, "Life is poetry. You are an apprentice to the feminine and the spirit of the bard. You are going beyond all that to a great love, a great awakening of all the circles. You will be a new kind of teacher. I will work with you until the year 2000, and then you are on your own. We are one. I am there beside you, glowing, alive, becoming real."

My spirit wife spoke directly to my heart. She was the muse. "I am not from the Pleiades," she said. "I am from the Central Sun, where you are originally from and to where you are returning. You do not know your future and do not have to. Come with me to another place that exists on Earth but that is beyond your consciousness. There you are the Source; you do not have to create. I am the teacher of what you have not learned on Earth."

I felt like Dante with Beatrice. She took over writing this book, my beloved wife. "I exist in a complementary reality," she said, "and have come to join with you so you can learn twice as much. I am from a parallel world and complete your experience here in time.

"What I bring is an experience of other dimensions—dimensions that are both like and unlike yours. This is for your survival, so listen. In me, the stars and Earth are not separate, and I am giving birth to aspects of yourself. Your three sons are the healing of your male side. The daughter is your pride and joy, the developing female. Your sons are strong like you and want to know their father. You are the father of form and a healthy discipline for them.

"Embrace your sons," she went on. "Share with them

your leadership, your love, and your connection to all things. They know you as the blue hummingbird. You see, we are just getting reacquainted with you. We've been away, traveling apart from each other. Time is ending now, so we can reunite. Then you will experience a transformation of matter and energy such as you have never experienced. Together we go into the unknown."

Was I hallucinating? No, this woman felt more real to me than the cats and owls that helped to guide me in the physical world. She was their medicine purified, a true medicine woman. In her demeanor, I recognized my friend Dawn Eagle Woman from Wyoming.

Dawn was one of my closest friends. In one of her vision quests, she stood in a medicine wheel while a vast storm approached. "If this land is to become Soaring Eagle Ranch, then do not let it rain in this wheel!" she declared to the storm. It rained all around the wheel but not on that sacred ground. She later bought Soaring Eagle Ranch in Wyoming, a refuge for people and animals, a place to begin a real community and a real bonding with the Earth.

On an earlier vision quest, Dawn had been frustrated one morning, thinking she had not gotten her medicine name and that she had missed some important lessons. Her teacher saw her doubt and told her to turn around. Behind her were twelve eagles soaring against the rising sun. That's when she became Dawn Eagle Woman. I loved her fierce and gentle soul.

My spirit wife reminded me of a past life in Wyoming that I had shared with Dawn. In that life, Dawn Eagle Woman was the chief of our tribe, and I was a shaman. We held council and loved to laugh at ourselves. She had been

my spirit wife on Earth in that life. In my mind, I returned
to Soaring Eagle Ranch to reconnect to Dawn Eagle
Woman's memory through the air, the rocks, the medicine
wheel.

"Regardless of your sexuality in this life, I have come
to show you new forms of play," she said, "a new quality of
relationship that is sensual in a healing way. I am another
yourself. Tell the people that the hummingbirds and the
lightning path are coming. The people will soon be firmly
rooted on the Earth, looking in bliss at the skies. We are the
Wayshowers of the Heart. Don't try to understand now.
All this will be shown and understood intuitively." I held
her and smelled the roselike fragrance of a wildflower I
could not name.

"The Fifth World is opening," I heard Dawn Eagle
Woman say. "Look at the Black Sun, the comet that is coming. See Nibiru and await the birth of the divine child, the
man in you in another form. You do not know what reality
you will be playing in next; it is so different from where you
are now. In the Fifth World, all your knowing will be translated as feeling, recognition, and love.

"It is difficult to describe the Fifth World," she went on.
"In seven years, you will know it thoroughly and move into a
community in the Four Corners region. For now, look to the
Pleiades and the renewed connection to your Mother Earth.
Tell people not to try to understand but to act as if they were
mountains. Indigenous people feel the spirit of the mountain
near where they grew up. Hold that mountain in your heart
and see me as the valley of your dreams."

Dawn Eagle Woman continued: "The mountains of your
heart and the valley of my soul are joined in the sacred pipe

and the medicine wheel. This is our wedding. The dark man
in you has become an Earth steward, and the prince has
become a soul teacher. I am the princess who has shaken
hands with the dragon. I am at your side. I am your anima,
both light and dark, and I will root your soul."

"Who are the blue hummingbirds?" I asked her.

"They are the keepers of your soul's records, the Keepers
of Tradition. They will inaugurate the Fifth World when
enough souls have adapted to the intensity of their heart
opening in balance with the Earth. The animals are leaving
to return to their world. Animals connect us to different star
systems. They are returning home. They see through different lenses. Don't try to hold a hummingbird in your hand—
you'll kill it. You do not have to die again in this life because
you are becoming original. Your new life will be gentle. One
world is dying, and a new one is being born."

"What is hummingbird medicine?" I asked.

"The consciousness of the dark made light, the joy that
eludes humankind. It is the story of how to walk out of
time's clothing in ecstasy."

"What is my soul's work?"

"To become the essence of the heart on Earth. We are
joined now. Your next books will be about what happens
after the sacred marriage. Lightning may strike you twice.

"Lightning conducts electricity to the center of the
Earth," she went on. "This electromagnetic energy comes
from the impregnation of the Earth by the stars. We come
from the stars, most of us. I am a part of you that remained
here at the center, the *axis mundi*. You sacrificed your Ram
for me. You broke from your mother to know me.

"We came here from many galaxies, planets, stars, and

star systems: Andromeda, Aldebaran, Auriga, Alpha Centauri, Arcturus, Regulus, Procyon, Orion, Lyra, Venus, and Zeta Reticuli. The stellar bodies do not exist outside your consciousness. You *are* the stars, and they are you. The names are not important. We may not all come from the same place, but we come from the same Source. Our genetic material has been very mixed, interbred with extraterrestrials and earthlings of all races.

"You came to Santa Fe and the Four Corners region of New Mexico to witness the lightning, struck by its metaphor for your coming to Earth and your return to the stars. The center of the Earth is safe and protected. The Earth is strong enough to be impregnated. At the center of the Earth is a silence that can contain everything. It is woven of all your feelings, stories, and memories.

"May you and the children of the Earth feel safe and call Earth your home," Dawn Eagle Woman told me. "Build strong soul containers—pottery filled with the integrity of your Mother and the lightning will of your Father. Talk to Grandmother Turtle. The birds, animals, and spirits are her ears. Create a soul. Risk being filled by Spirit and allow the humming tension to begin. Find the inner Magi, your imagination, and birth the divine essence that wants to incarnate within you."

Then she concluded, "I send you the Black Sun teachings that will be the end of your book—the end and beginning of my message to the Teachers of the Heart."

After I wrote down these last words, I went for a walk. Two ravens circled—one clockwise, the other counterclockwise. They said, "All is finished. Keep life simple."

The next day, I discovered that the ravens had dropped
five feathers, and I heard them cackling from inside the trees,
guiding me to dozens of dove and sparrow feathers. As I
turned in gratitude to leave, a blue hummingbird feather
fell from the sky. I caught it and held it to my heart.

Then a black butterfly with white spots lit next to me
and walked onto the outstretched index finger of my right
hand. I felt a rush go through the male side of my body. I
heard huge wings beating over my head, but no birds were
in sight. The black butterfly stayed on my hand for an hour,
walking me through the medicine wheel.

First I faced the west, the black, place of my shadow,
place of inner death and transformation. Turning to the
north, the white, I felt the union of opposites, the birth of
the medicine man, and the snows of many winters. Then I
turned all the way around and faced the south, the red, place
of gentle fire and community and a new circle of friends. Last
I faced east, the yellow, place of the golden union of myself
with creation and the cosmos. I felt the vastness and great-
ness of living.

My spirit drifted upward. From a place in the clouds, I
looked down the *axis mundi*, the staff of my body, and saw
the underworld, the land of the midnight sun, and embraced
it. Then I climbed the shamanic sacred tree, looked at the
heavenly world, and embraced the sun, my own essence.
Finally, turning inward to the center, I yelled, "I am that I
am! I have found the presence of the divine in myself, and I
fully incarnate on Earth as a bridge to all worlds and dimensions. I am the mandala of life turning like fire in the sky,
dreaming the world anew."

The black butterfly turned around in a circle and flew off

my hand. I heard, "The past is over. You are healed. These are the teachings of the Black Lodge and the blue hummingbird in your heart."

Dawn Eagle Woman had connected me to my anima, my spirit wife, whose presence is always with me. My spirit wife is a true partner, and I love her as my feminine half. As a result of this experience, I began to spend time in Wyoming at Soaring Eagle Ranch with wild horses and lions.

COMMUNITY

I used to sing for wild lions. In Wyoming, there is a valley of large stones where a lone mountain lion lives. I heard his song while sitting in a cave that was lined in petroglyphs made by ancient hunters. The lion was searching for a mate, a family, a community in the wild. I went to him.

As the song came to me, a large mountain lion walked up and sat a few yards away. He felt the overtones from my voice ringing through his body. Tears rolled from both our eyes. When he heard the last note, the lion got up and walked away. By the next year, that lion had found a mate, and she was pregnant.

The mountain lion gave me a great gift. He helped me have the courage to find the leader within and to ask for a mate. Later, I began to lead groups of people in new forms of creative expression. The lion would come to me in dreams and tell me to speak my truth, stand by my convictions, and move at the pace of the slowest person in any group. After that, I learned to solve communication problems by finding the potential leader in the other person and encouraging them to speak out.

I talked to Native American elders, kahuna teachers from Hawaii, and aboriginal matriarchs, and they all said to me, "Follow the lion heart. Never be far from the land you love. Ask the Old Ones how to live in community and find peace." I learned from them that the only true power is spiritual power and that communion—relationship to all life—is the best way to be human. I was told that we are here to walk in beauty, follow the dance of the sun, and help create a heaven on Earth. I was told to go on a vision quest and ask, "Who am I?" and to fast for a clear perception.

On my vision quest, I saw millions of people leaving coastal cities and moving inland. I saw large migrations to smaller communities that emphasized art, storytelling, and music. I had dreams of tidal waves, earthquakes, comets, and a brilliant new pole star. I felt the psychic split between those who lived in the past and feared change—those who were lost in the cultural trance—and those who dreamed of wheels, lodges, and sanctuaries.

The new communities were called centers of rejuvenation because the world was falling apart and they were intended to help hold it together. In the old world, governments collapsed and banks faltered. People who chose to stay in that world lost touch with the land and created disease and disharmony.

The new communities had many children, and their members were marked by their tolerance for diversity. Their mutual commitment to a dream of interrelationship made the center hold in harmony. They were committed to building trust through learning how to listen. I saw Grandmother Turtle teaching the women a new way of partnership. Women were often the teachers of men. That was my vision, and I knew that my destiny was to be included in such a dream.

In Wyoming, I lived for days with a herd of twenty-two wild horses. The leader, a stud named Silver Trail, grew to like me. He came to my tipi one morning to wake me up. I caressed him and all the other horses. I learned their form of communication—a kind of telepathy—and in the process, my own instincts became better integrated.

Though I was aware of being in a human body, I felt more like a horse than a human. They awakened my power to be free, unbridled, balanced sensually in my body. They taught me fierceness, speed, loyalty, and balance. The stud personally taught me how to be a leader in action. He was wise, gentle, and nurturing.

Returning to Santa Fe, I planted a vegetable garden with eighteen varieties of herbs and hundreds of wildflowers, irises, and tulips. I searched for mugwort, wormwood, and wild sage. I went on long psychic "trips" to learn the uses of each plant, and I drew symbols that were given to me by the spirits of each flower.

I planted twelve trees, one for each month, and constructed three medicine wheels on the property I was caretaking. I even built a Cretan maze, following the labyrinthine path each morning to balance the left and right hemispheres of my brain. In the center of each wheel I laid cornmeal, tobacco, fruit, and gemstones as an offering to the Great Mystery. I walked around the wheels three-and-a-half times, praying for harmony so that the land and I would always be one. Every morning I greeted the sun, and every evening I saluted the stars, and spirit-traveled.

After a while, a rhythm began to develop. Each season was reencoding itself in my body. I experienced states of bliss on new and full moons. Animals came closer and closer to the house. I started to collect and make rugs, baskets, pottery, weavings, soap, and drums. Life became simpler but demanded that I be very present with loving thoughts all the time. If I had a festering negative thought, birds would fling themselves at the windows, the wind would become fierce, and it wouldn't rain for days.

Gratitude became my purpose in living. As an act of personal empowerment, I began giving many gifts to people. I started my service to creation in thanks for the gracefulness of my life. After one ceremony to honor the sacred Four Directions, a double rainbow formed in the sky. One afternoon, two eagles flew over the front yard, and their shadows made the sign of the *vesica piscis* on the Earth. Hawks started sitting on the mailbox. A snake shed its skin directly in front of the medicine wheel in the south. Ravens gathered on the roof to chatter, and my heart burst with thanks.

During this time, a family in Santa Fe, the Bennetts, adopted me. We gathered on the full moon for feasts. Their children and I played on a trampoline and on volleyball and basketball courts. I played like I had never played as a child. We traveled as an extended family to Arizona, Colorado, Hawaii, and other places.

This family's ability as a group to mediate conflicts and disputes healed my soul. They had proper boundaries and were exceedingly generous. I had never loved people so much in my life. Their unconditional love changed forever my view of relationships. They taught me love, companionship, and the strength of vulnerability. We could discuss any topic, and they held no judgments. I even cried on their shoulders. They also cooked the finest meals I had ever eaten.

When I got into a minor accident during this time, I realized that my whole perspective on life had been altered. After another car rammed into mine, I remained calm.

"What is the lesson here?" I asked myself, and I heard, "Love these gracious people, even though they hit your car."

In spite of the fact that the accident had not been my fault, I wrote those people a check to help with the damage to their car and told them, "You can trust me. Here is my phone number. You will be taken care of, even if you don't have insurance." No police came, and there was no drama. I felt a deep sense of peace, and the people were greatly bewildered.

Every morning, I took a walk near my home to the tree the ravens slept in. I asked Raven to bring me feathers to give away, and the birds always left a gift. I also enjoyed visiting the magpies on the fence, listening to them chatter and gossip. They would tease and yell at me to leave.

If friends came to visit, I would give them a tour of the rabbit holes or show them where to find the mushrooms that grew in circles. I would ask the sage if it wanted to be picked. I would ask the devas how I could help them in the garden. In my garden, I learned that every plant comes from a different star; they were "starseeded" just like human beings.

When I healed my fear of spiders, they made intricate webs all over my home to teach me the ways of Spider Woman. They made it clearer to me how we humans are a beautiful facet in the intricate web of all things. They taught me how to be empowered through accepting my true fate. "Have loving thoughts so your web will be strong," they told me. "If you resist the web, you might get caught in it." Sometimes they crawled on top of me if I was not getting their messages. I began to listen, making Native American dream catchers and reweaving a new life inside my own body.

My soul shouted at the sky, "Teach me how to be a rain-

maker, Thunderbeings! Teach me how to do the rain dance.
I want to learn!" Every time it rained, I walked outside.
"Teach me now!" I would say. Then it would rain a great deal
for awhile, often only on my roof. Rain is a gift of cleansing.
Between 1992 and 2012, we will all be in the midst of the
Great Purification. All of our issues will surface to be cleared.
This is the great clearing of the astral body of man and
Earth.

Before I even moved into this house, I knew that the
Thunderbeings had thrown lightning into the front yard.
The previous tenant had built a pyramid on the lawn deco-
rated with objects from all over the world. When he finished
erecting it, a lightning bolt struck and incinerated his creation. He then found an owl and buried it with reverence near
the garage. I moved in shortly thereafter.

For a year afterward, my dreams took me all over the
globe. I bought a map and placed pins where I had gone
dreaming the night before. Altogether, I placed pins in
twenty locations: Bali; Kenya; Egypt; Greece; Tibet; Kuaui;
Bear Butte, South Dakota; Serpent Mound, Ohio; Mount
Shasta; Belize; Malta; Ayer's Rock and Byron Bay, Australia;
Iona, Scotland; Glastonbury; the Yucatán; the Four Corners
region; Mount Fuji, Japan; and Lake Titicaca, Peru. I sent
fibers from my own body to these places on the planetary
body. These locations were all sacred repositories for the
ancient wisdom and records of the Earth. They were sites of
initiation. I began to dream the world anew, performing ceremonies in my astral body at these specific sites. I kept jour-
nals of my trips around the Earth, hoping one day I could
make these journeys physically.

The atlas in my home became filled with marks. Circles
and Xs were drawn where I had dreamed that a future com-

munity would be created. I made a grid, a network of future centers all over the planetary surface. My intention in the Dreamtime was to help people move to one of these centers at the right time; this became my planetary work. After that, strangers began to call from around the world, asking where I felt they could buy land to build a community. The dream was manifesting.

A year after my vision quest, I replanted the garden, and a black starling came. The apparently sick bird walked beside me during the whole seeding process. She jumped and hobbled, grazing my feet. I gave her water to drink but felt her life force ebbing away. When I finished planting, she died. I buried that blackbird with great respect.

Then one night, the same bird arrived in a dream and said, "A seed must die and be buried in the dark. A soul must be buried in the darkness of the Earth, to bear roots and reach the sun. I sacrificed myself for the seed. The plants sacrifice themselves for you. Life lives from life. The seed of love you plant now will bear much fruit in a later period of your life. Be content with what you have."

After that incident, the devas in the garden began to talk to me. "You are here on Earth to create consciousness, to be curious, to ask questions, to take care of creation by listening to your heart and responding with a balanced mind," they said. "Do not believe that evil exists or that people are bad. That is an improper use of the mind, a human illusion. You are the reed that must be played in order for you to be happy. Whenever you doubt your connection to creation, hear the music of hidden things. Hear your destiny calling to you from the silence. Believe in yourself. You have a spiritual destiny. Let the ants teach you patience in gathering."

I asked the devas about community, and I heard them

say, "Community is the path home. A world of love and abundance is not a fantasy; it is the way things are. Touch the earth to know your origins. Learn to work with creation as a family. Children need a gentler birth. Conceive your children in clarity and conscious union. Women must teach men how to be. Men are afraid of the power of women. Women must teach men to trust again, to create new forms of economy, new forms of planting and gathering, nurturing and partnership. Girls must do quests for their animal allies and sit in rainbow lodges when they have their first blood. Menstruation, the wise wound, must be celebrated.

"Men will learn to share wealth and power cooperatively," the devas went on. "They will build their dreams through permaculture, bioremediation, solar design, yurts, domes . . ." The devas combed my mind for examples. "Men will create new solar rituals, new forms of art, storytelling, and music. They will have morning clearings of all their guilt and negativity for the good of the whole community.

"Men will learn to love other men," they said. "A true brotherhood will arise that is empowering and inspirational. New rites of passage will help boys to become responsible members of the community. They will learn that the hunter and the hunted are one and how to respect women and elders again. Men will follow the hummingbird and nurture the soul of the land together in groups.

"Many communities will be centers for rejuvenation, like cells in the Earth organism," the devas continued, "and you will participate in these developments. New light and sound work will be discovered through group activity. People will feel as one, even though they are on independent paths. There will be many different stages of evolution in the new communities. People will have more respect for diversity, and outrageousness will thrive. When you share garden duties, you will have more time to play. With that free time, you will direct a new form of theater. People will dance the planets and perform new myths. You will travel in tents as large troupes, creating new forms of participatory performance.

"Help people tell their own stories," the devas admonished me. "Your work in this new medium is why you have incarnated. You will help many to become dancing healers again as they embrace their innate creativity. Bring harmony and integrity to your play. That is what brings you maximum joy in any incarnation. Enjoy life, but first take care of the garden."

Gradually, I even started to resemble the devas physically. As I tilled the earth and got my hands full of mud and compost, my hair curled in waves, my eyes twinkled, and my body became lighter and more ethereal. I began to think and act like a deva, becoming more mischievous and energetic. Their consciousness and mine became one. They told me to collect stones from anthills and paint them, placing the stones in rattles. When I played the rattles, the devas said, they would help others to heal. I was filled with a deep reverence for life. In becoming my true self, I had become a true elf.

I stayed awake one evening with my lover, staring up at the Pleiades. I saw my inner guides, Gwynhwyrr and George, sitting beside me. "We are going to have a great adventure this life with you," declared George excitedly. "This has only been the preparation, the beginning of your training. We want you to travel, basing yourself here and . . ."

I interrupted. "I, Foster, am so happy to be right here

in this moment. I do not have to go anywhere. I love you all, my seen and unseen family. I am happy to be alive. That is all that is important."

As I said this, I saw all the many aspects of myself—all my projections ensouling the world—coming toward me, and I said to the returning host, "It's time for all of you to come together inside, as a community of soul."

All my past and future lives formed a circle, with me in the center. I could feel my soul, the angelic self, God/ Goddess, entering the substance of my body. I felt every cell undergo a solar integration. "May all the aspects of self be embraced and rewoven now. I am ready!" my heart declared.

Immediately, lights from a multitude of objects—tables, walls, plants, trees—started to return to my body. I felt a greenish light from within the Earth enter my solar plexus and heart. All the chakra wheels inside my body began to turn and light up the pathways of my form. I witnessed the Seven Sisters of the Pleiades enter and return to the sanctuary of my heart, balancing Orion, the Seven Hunters, and the Great Bear. I perceived all my male heroes—Taliesin, Robin of the Wood, Herne, Michael, and others—stand before me and join my soul to a larger community of men. I could feel my hands burning as the lines in my palms changed positions. I felt my destiny changing.

I put those hands through my lover's long hair and felt my spirit wife join with my soul. What was once outside me had now become the fabric of a larger heart. All my parts had come home. I sat quietly, breathing in my chair, and became the world and the stars. Outside, there was nothing but the vast, universal Self beating to the rhythm of a hummingbird's soul.

DIALOGUES WITH THE SOUL

I hear the language of the soul as a dialogue. Here are some moments in our eternal conversation.

I tell my lovers, "Because you are the way you are, I can be myself." Whoever they are and however they act, I still love them, even though they may have broken my heart. It is a gift of love to go through heartbreak, to see yourself and go beyond suffering to the core of someone else.

What lies on the other side of love is not fear but a lack of tools. I feel grateful to those who do not hug me when they first meet me. They shake my hand; they have good boundaries. This is more precious to me than an undifferentiated hug. Hugs are often needy. Sometimes people want to be hugged in order to be validated. If their intent is not clear, your energy is drained and you wonder what has happened. It is better to find trust in your own intention to love and embrace another.

Slow down. The straight line to the self often leads nowhere. We can abolish straight lines and right angles because they only teach rigidity. The straight line between two points is *not* always the shortest route; there are many obstacles and circuitous paths that lead to the center of the soul.

Many spiritual devotees and teachers have no soul; they have let go of it, thinking it was their ego. They make sacred vows and read sacred texts and are profoundly connected to a higher consciousness but have lost their souls, their emotions. Some of these people even stop admitting that they have feelings, yet they exude feelings though they may not perceive them. God wants us to articulate both the heights and depths of our emotions.

The greatest tool for learning the lessons of emotion is falling in love—with a person, an experience, a tree, a home, a child. When we first become attached to something, we begin to learn to love. Many people are attached to nothingness, emptiness, and even that can be a kind of soul love. A Zen Buddhist staring at a black drapery may know a great love for the ecstasy of the moment, the blackness of the void. If you give him a flower as a gift, he will keep that flower alive with his love for a long time.

To love even an object with great dedication and feeling is to imbue that object with consciousness. Forget all books, paths, and teachings and find out who and what you really love. Conjure up a rose, a flame, a face, a blackness. There is emptiness in loving, as well as desire and attraction. It is the same desire and attraction that created this world. It is the same desire and attraction that made you want to surround yourself with sensations. It was the very force that prompted you to want to experience being human. Celebrate your desires as a reflection of the Source.

You wait, expecting someone else to tell you how to live, how to pray, how to love yourself. You expect lovers to return your love, but they don't return it. In that circumstance, your expectation is your lover. Your expectation is a surrogate love. Love your expectations until you are tired of them and they of you. If you are too attached to them, your expectations become your nemesis, your "enemies."

You can even become needy for others to mirror your own faults. You may need people to hurt you in order to punish yourself. After many times doing this, you either die or begin laughing. I have often laughed hard because the thing or person I wanted did not want me back. They did not have the tools to care for me. Then sometimes, because of the way they were, I gave up wanting to love and found love wanting me. The heart chose me as a path through which to open. Love came to me when I had lost all hope of finding it.

The ego, mind, and personality talk so much about love. But remember that what you truly desire also desires you. It is a law of creation. When you have sensual or lusty dreams, do they always materialize? No, and when they do, it is because your soul has prepared for their arrival and wanted to rescue love in this way. Life can only give you healing.

"Then why so much pain?"

Because you believe pain exists.

"But I feel the pain."

Because you created it. Right thinking is to ask for something else.

"But it is still there."

We experience pain when we judge loneliness or separation as a bad thing. There is nothing bad about separation. As soon as we finally separate, we naturally begin to rejoin.

Judgment keeps separation from completing its task.

"What if the pain has materialized as a bodily disease or ailment of some kind?"

Then you have learned to manifest thoughts into the physical. Remember how you did it, and do it again with a different thought.

"When I began to heal, I drew more needy people to me. Why?"

Many have forgotten to do anything for themselves. Many want to be healed without doing any work. Nothing permanent or worthwhile is achieved without effort.

"I lost myself helping others; that is what people tell me."

What is your motivation? To scare yourself back into old patterns? Did you not have the tools to nurture yourself?

"Who am I?"

A light without form, a trick of the eye, a sounding. We are not solid. We dissolve all day. There are moments when you are invisible, when you are dreaming nothing.

"Why do I dream?"

To keep the waking mind from believing it is the only one that exists.

"Won't I stop dreaming when I am enlightened or more spiritually evolved?"

When you stop dreaming, you stop existing. If you want not to exist, there are other ways of doing that.

"Why would I not want to be? Why would I not want to dream life?"

Because you do not love your depressions and moods as a gathering of soul force. You may not want to be because you do not want to live in the spiritual here-and-now on Earth. None of the other dimensions offer the opportunities you

have here. There is a heaven right here on Earth, a Garden
of Eden right here on Earth. See it; that is the promise you
made to God.

"Why am I afraid to change?"

Because there is nothing to change. What is changing are
only your feelings, your thoughts about the river. The river is
a metaphor for life. How do we carry the river inside us while
still being conscious of its force? Change is of the Goddess
and is very still. Change is a form of mimicry. You have
always been the silence. The soul changes as it emerges from
within the stillness and is felt.

"Why are you so vague and obscure?"

There is much to digest in life. Life needs a paradox to
undo itself. What is vague for one person contains the whole
seed for another. It is a question of feeling deeply, of knowing
life just as it is.

"Why do we want to change the Earth to heal it?"

The Earth asked you to come here to witness her birth
through you. You are only the surface, while the center of the
Earth is untouched, an egg untrammeled by humankind, a
source of creation.

"Who are you to know these things?"

I am a star traveler, in your time for the moment to experience desire as love. I came here to be touched.

"Why is life so hard?"

Because we have not grown into the frequency of the
wood. We have not become its hardness.

"If we become the hard wood, what happens?"

We cease to be hard.

"Does matter change as our thoughts change?"

It only appears that we can change form. After death, you
may become lighter and lighter until you dissolve into the

All. Then, when you feel a tugging to leave the All, you
return to form again. While you are in form, you have never
left the All. You never change; you gather life into yourself—
every memory, every event, every thought—and your soul
contains it all forever. Your soul creates everything in the
image of the All in order to know itself.

"Isn't that a process of becoming?"

Not when you return things to love. They vibrate with
the center of the Earth and the center of the galaxy. All our
souls are being returned to love as one.

"What happens then?"

Life becomes transparent. Transformation is trans-
parency. You are here to return everything to love. You are
an invisible awakening of love in form. Someone larger
is dreaming you, dancing your form into existence from
another dimension with great loving care.

"Who are the Elohim? The creator gods?"

They are beings much like you, versed in creating
worlds. You are becoming Elohim.

"What is channeling?"

It is communicating light, reading available information. It is not important in itself. It comes through wanting
to become yourself, humbly acknowledging the Source and
seeing that it is you in another form.

"What is beauty?"

Love's contemplation of itself.

"When will I feel beautiful?"

When you love the depression, the negative, as something building a vessel, a cauldron of water in which to see
yourself.

"How many worlds are there?"

Countless and none. You are the worlds; the galaxies

are in your body. A human being contains every metal, all
144 elements—everything that exists in the universe.

"What is distance?"

An arbitrary aberration that human beings perceive.
Your eyes focus on distance, but it is not real.

"What is existence?"

The leaves turning over on their backs. The face of the
wind slapping your cheek. The cold touch of a winter stream.
The loneliness of the patriarchy or of the matriarchies that
nurtured but forgot to listen to the contributions of men.
The emptiness a flower feels when it is unacknowledged.
Your running away from yourself to the loneliest corner
to make loneliness a blessing and turn it into a pleasure.

"What is pleasure?"

Pleasure is admitting that you are nurtured by the universe from a seed to a form.

"What is beyond light?"

New forms, new joys, a grand playing.

"What is the fifth dimension, and is it beyond form?"

It is nondual, neither this nor that. It is where you are
coming from when you project yourself here.

"What is loneliness?"

Loneliness is not expressing your being with enough clarity and forcefulness, so that you cannot receive a response. It
is thinking you are above life when you are below it. Many of
your aspects are actually subterranean—below consciousness.
Your reptilian brain is still submerged. You long to know
darkness, the Black Madonna. Look deeper into the core of
this planet. It is a jewel in the darkness, with a core as light
and bright as the sun.

"Why do we have a sun?"

To orient ourselves to the Source.

"Why do we have a moon?"

The moon is like the sun when you leave this world. She is the reflection of instinct. As the Mother of Form, she can embrace you. Luna is sentient and alive. Her teaching is that of surrender. You call the moon the "Goddess Sin" and then make the lunar goddess "sinful" on Earth. You sin by not reflecting.

"What are Jupiter's attributes?"

The mastery of how to play and the memory of how to play without encumbrance.

"What will happen in the next years?"

The galactic cycles of time, the Mayan calendar, all tell of a future. The real future is a question, a becoming. In reality, there is no future. Probabilities can create enslavement. The future is a creative act and is not important. The soul is emerging out of time.

"Isn't the soul made up of many voices?"

Souls were created to feel the Earth. They are many timbred. They can agitate or bring joy. An essence is beyond the soul, and it feels, too. The jaguar soul teaches the proper way to be on the Earth: the soul with a hummingbird in its heart.

"What is service?"

No one serves anything. Compassion is to not see anyone as separate from you. Teach the tools of nurturing the self into existence. To reincarnate soul and God in your body— that is your task. There is a time to not do service, to stop and go inward and serve the self. You face all your selfishness, and then you serve again.

"Why don't we appreciate ourselves?"

Appreciation is a gift. It comes from looking back at yourself and the work you've done. No one can really appreciate themselves because appreciation comes from another place where you already exist as one greatly loved.

"What is self-acceptance?"

A loneliness, a need to be wanted. No one has to want you. Embrace the lack of love in the world, the darkness, and evolve through all the hardships you create. Then open to a new place, a new home. This is the gateway. The heart that faces everything is full. You are beyond acceptance. Open your hands to another like yourself. Do you accept yourself then?

"No, not always."

Ask for something greater than self-acceptance.

"Greater than the self?"

Yes. Love and the pure feeling of creation.

The soul is a living dialogue, with both sides interacting equally. We want to go beyond teacher-student relationships here. There will be no more schooling on Earth. As your soul fully incarnates, you will be filled with the memory of everything, and you will move slowly beyond all limits. You will still have boundaries and experience solitude, but all you will need to do is play compassionately. You will hear color and see sound as the devas do. You will become love, grace, the present moment, and then you will tell many stories. You will come into matter as lightning and stand firmly on the Earth, building your home with a strong new foundation.

*T*he journey I have taken you on is a celebration of life, the path of the hummingbird, a balancing of death with the rising of the midnight sun. Great changes are occurring in this world as we realign with an understanding of nonduality. We are seeing through a third eye the beauty and intricacy of the Web of Wyrd, the interdependency of all life on the medicine wheel. This is our homecoming. We are reawakening to the soul, our essential self, in matter. Lightning is striking the hummingbird in our hearts.

All my life, I have been deeply connected to the unconscious, engaging in dreamwork, trying to reveal the numinous to others. This work comes from the soul and uses me as its vehicle. Mediumistic abilities such as clairsentience, clairaudience, and communing with plants, animals, and spirits have been the norm in my life. I feel like the Katochoi, people in service to the God or Goddess who lived in cloisters and temples in voluntary seclusion in antiquity. I have been the Katochoi in many worlds, bringing into this life a full memory of other lives and simultaneous existences. This integration of knowledge into experience has been the storytelling of this book, the first thirty-three years of my life.

The central teaching of my life has been our relationship to our innermost soul and the seeking of the inner male in partnership and equality with the inner feminine. The sacred marriage of opposites has been my repeated initiation, even in my prebirth memories of being a twin. I have experienced nonduality, seen eternity in the transitory, and laughed at the humor of living in worlds both divine and banal.

Being hit by lightning awakened and refined my energies. The first explosive moments were followed by solitude, reflection, and discernment. During the months and years afterward, my depressions became helpful tools for dipping into the unconscious. Sometimes they created radical introversion, as well as new ideas, healthier responses, and longer cycles of play.

Eros, the divine child, is a symbol of the positive male initiator. The god in us has both a masculine and a feminine face, and they are both one and diversified. The star person learns to feel through experiencing human life. Epaphus, the Greek god of sensual touch, teaches us not to possess anyone or anything. Eros torches the soul in order to purify it. Such lessons are not easy in this world, but feeling is the true source of individuation.

It has not been easy feeling ordinary when I have been so showered by the gifts of Spirit. My greatest gift and teacher has been the Puer Aeternus, the spirit of eternal youth. He has taught this hummingbird how to explore his shadow, bond with his physical father, differentiate his inner feminine from that of his mother, discover his soul, and be initiated by the sun god within.

The puer introduced me to the Wise Old Man, with whom I have conversed within my psyche. My early dialogues with Christ, and later with aboriginal, Native American, and kahuna elders, helped make possible my later dialogue with my father when he had cancer. The Young Man and the Old Man have joined in eternal conversation in my soul, and they have helped me mature.

Wisdom comes through balancing logos and Eros, knowledge with the experience of the heart. My private healing sessions with others have been a source of constant surprise and joy. Work has helped me focus on the present and remain alert, challenged by the call to intimacy.

Because of its high vibrational frequency, the humming-bird is so close to death that its spirit can never be confined or it will die. With its rapidly beating heart and wings, it fertilizes the flowers, extracting the nectar of all things. I have had two near-death experiences and many little deaths in this lifetime. I have learned not to make a cult of beauty or aesthetics but to love apparent ugliness.

To integrate the ugliness inside the shadow, I had to undergo the difficult process of releasing my positive and negative mother complexes. I became a son and lover of the Great Mother, but I also had to learn to find my ordinary self and adapt to being human.

I thank life for this process. The here and now is the place to be. I am not here to save the world but to fully realize the self, the God incarnate, the collective birth of the Earth Child as love.

Love is both a mystery and an ordinary human event. The humility we learn through the process of loving holds us together in divine containers. Nature helps us build vessels that protect our deepest creative powers. Storytelling, paint-ing, poetry, writing, singing, dancing, geomancy, music, theater—these are the inspirations of our muses and our pur-pose in creating community. The greatest creativity comes from the depths when we stay with it long enough. Yet even the perfect creation has a flaw. We must love our imperfec-tions as our beauty and gather ourselves for the one who is to come, the one who embodies everything.

Embracing conflict allows the shadow to become vital, connected to healthy aggression and discernment. I was always at home in the heights, feeling eternal, but I asked the

horned god and the Mithraic bull to create a new man, an
Earth steward who would be torn apart and put together in
a new wild way. Eventually, the male in me became a new
individual whose purpose was to serve life.

The meetings with my spirit wife revealed profound
mysteries about the bridge between Earth and sky. Today,
I feel the jaguar of the south and the eagle of the north
helping to form the bridge we must all build on this con-
tinent. Now, the tribes and races are coming together after
the initiation of the shadow, and the unity of male and
female will signal the next phase of our evolution.

Mine is the story of Osiris, a new male mixed with the
androgyny of the man-woman shaman. He illumines both
sexes in order to integrate and marry them fully. The cup
of the soul contains the philosopher's stone. In Glastonbury,
I found my cup full of roses and insights into the return to
love and innocence. I had to journey to the lower self and to
Alcyone in the Pleiades to see the Black Lodge teachings and
to understand the saying "As above, so below." That is when
the blue hummingbirds drop their feathers in your heart.

The Ant People have taught me to be patient, to be a
child of Mother Earth, and to emerge into the Fourth World,
our present age, more fully, in order to see clearly in a dark
time, then to emerge consciously into the Fifth World of harmony among all beings. This is what happens when lightning strikes a hummingbird: acceleration and completion of
the past and the birth of a new species in another dimension.
I had to birth the union of dark and light, finding both Seth
and Osiris inside. My idealistic wish to do good when I was a
born-again Christian had to learn to cooperate with my dark,
aggressive masculinity.

Dreams lead the way to integration of the best and worst

in us. I grew to love the alchemy of my shadow and its eventual brightening in the mental union of opposites. Then came the red initiation, seeing life as it is. And last was union with the cosmos, the emergence into gold and beyond to a new color spectrum that we are just on the threshold of seeing. Just as we become familiar with one dimension or world, we enter a new one, vastly different, and it changes us forever.

I talk to the universal self in everything—plants, animals, devas, fetishes, angels, stars—all of creation in its original instructions. I have met Horus as my new personality, the divine child, and Old Man Horus, my guide. During this process, my own feelings of inferiority and the wonderful mistakes I have made have proven to be some of the greatest gifts.

In my journey, I have found the pearl of the soul, the cosmos within, and have never left that perception of life. It is, in fact, the silence that no one has ever left. I hid that pearl during my temple lives but emerge with it now to share it with you. Perhaps I have found the gold too early, and more of my inferior sides will come to light as a result. If so, I look forward to the continuing unfoldment.

God has fallen back into the womb, into the Mother, to become conscious in us. She/He emerges from below. We are opening to the soul, to the God self and beyond—and apparently at great price. God is now incarnating fully in matter, and nothing is the same as it has been. Our old beliefs, attachments, and healing practices are all falling away. Our broken hearts are opening in a new way. The rips and wounds in us have allowed God to emerge. God is being born in us as the divine child. There is an emerging maturity in the loving parents of this world.

One of the greatest things to learn is how to laugh at ourselves and not be too serious. Laughter is the root of all hope. In one pronunciation, the Pleiades sounds like *Play*-ades, whereas Sirius is very *serious* in its mysteries. We are now moving into a new cycle of balance between playfulness and seriousness. We are here to be flexible, listening to the fires, the Spirit Keepers of the Four Directions, and to love the lower and upper gods equally. Then we can manifest our dreams of unconditional love and begin lives of service in the world.

God/Goddess is always here, whether we call or not. As Rumi says in a poem called "Be Melting Snow" (from *Open Secret*), "God is in the look of your eyes, in the thought of looking, nearer to you than yourself or things that have happened to you. There's no need to go outside. Be melting snow. Wash yourself of yourself. A white flower grows in the quietness. Let your tongue become that flower."

I feel both my limits and my limitlessness, the marriage of the scoundrel and the gypsy in me and the marriage of the divine king and queen. Initiation in dreams is both bland and numinous. Life is a paradox, and we must live that paradox between the gates, passing freely through all states at the moment of full consciousness. We must surrender into integrity, loving our bodies for their dimensional transitions. Let us feel our bodies, resting as we go through this global awakening.

So much feeling rises up from the superabundance of my heart to you. The archangel Gabriel, revealer of divine messages, wanted me to write this book with pleasure. Gabriel came to Mary to teach her how to surrender, and to Daniel in the lion's den to interpret dreams, and to Zechariah to tell of the coming of John the Baptist.

Gabriel is the teacher of opening the heart to a personal and collective rebirth from 1992 to 2013. Open your heart to receive Khidr, the green man. He will connect you to the ocean, the rain, purification, the whales and dolphins who teach of a new community.

Welcome to the lunar realms of cycles, the rainbow bridges of trust, to explore the spiritual rebirth of the teacher, leader, and healer who reside inside everyone. Let yourself be ravished. Fill the cup of human kindness. Include all worlds within yourself and an acceptance of the new amid tears of release.

Everything is available now for evolution into kindness and mindfulness. Now we await the midnight sun and a new dawn. Let our new communities unite chaos and order into "wholarchies," mandalas and *woman*dalas, circles of elders and young people—all sharing, all included.

I have shared my old man, young man, child, parent, and my inner community of Self with you. May we be both endarkened and enlightened as the grandmothers and grandfathers pass their wisdom through our cells. Let our adventures begin in gratitude, and may we all express our stories. Everything is divine and holy.

To all our relations. And, as the Maya say, *"In Lak'ech: I am another yourself."*

Bly, Robert. *Iron John: A Book About Men.* Reading, MA: Addison Wesley Publishing, 1990.

Bradshaw, John E. *Healing the Shame That Binds You.* Deerfield Beach, FL: Health Communication, 1988.

Clow, Barbara Hand. *Chiron: Rainbow Bridge Between the Inner and Outer Planets.* St.Paul: Llewellyn Publications, 1987.

———. *Signet of Atlantis: War in Heaven Bypass.* Santa Fe, NM: Bear & Company, 1992.

de Rohan, Ceanne. *Right Use of Will.* Albuquerque, NM: One World Publications, 1984.

Ellis, Normandi. *Awakening Osiris: A New Translation of the Egyptian Book of the Dead.* Grand Rapids, MI: Phane Press, 1988.

Franz, Marie-Louise von. *The Golden Ass of Apuleius.* Boston: Shambhala Publications, 1970.

———. *Puer Aeternus.* Boston: Sigo Press, 1970.

Halifax, Joan. *Shaman: The Wounded Healer.* London: Thames and Hudson, 1982.

Hillman, James. *A Blue Fire.* New York: Harper & Row, 1987.

Jung, Carl Gustav. *Mysterium Coniunctionis.* Vol. 14, *Collected Works* of C.G. Jung. Translated by R.F.C. Hull. Princeton: Princeton University Press, 1963.

———. *Psychology of Alchemy.* Vol. 12, *Collected Works* of C.G. Jung. Translated by R.F.C. Hull. Princeton: Princeton University Press, 1953.

———. *Synchronicity: An Acausal Connecting Principle.* Princeton: Princeton University Press, 1973.

Lerner, Isha, and Mark Lerner. *Inner Child Cards*. Santa Fe, NM: Bear & Company, 1992.

Manitonquat. *Return to Creation*. Spokane, WA: Bear Tribe Publishing, 1991.

Richardson, Alan. *Earth God Rising: The Return of Male Mysteries*. St.Paul: Llewellyn Publications, 1990.

Rilke, Rainer Maria. *Sonnets to Orpheus*. Translated by David Young. Middleton, CN: Wesleyan University Press, 1987.

_____. *Letters to a Young Poet*. Translated by Stephen Mitchell. Random House, 1984.

Rumi, Jelaluddin. *Feeling the Shoulder of the Lion*. Translated by Colman Barks. Putney, VT: Threshold Books, 1991.

_____. *Open Secret*. Translated by John Moyne and Coleman Barks. Putney, VT: Threshold Books, 1984.

Sams, Jamie, and David Carson. *Medicine Cards*. Santa Fe, NM: Bear & Company, 1988.

Sitchin, Zechariah. *The Twelfth Planet*. Santa Fe, NM: Bear & Company, 1991.

Spilsbury, Ariel, and Michael Bryner. *The Mayan Oracle*. Santa Fe, NM: Bear & Company, 1992.

Tolkien, J.R.R. *The Lord of the Rings*. New York: Ballantine Books, 1967.

Woodman, Marion. *The Ravished Bridegroom: Masculinity in Women*. Toronto: Inner City Books, 1990.

*F*oster Perry is a spiritual teacher, artist, ceremonial leader, and caretaker of the soul. He lives in solitude, writing, counseling, and singing from his home in Santa Fe, New Mexico. He has studied with learned elders, shamans, and healers. After graduating from Georgetown University, he studied art, design, film, and dance. As the founding director of the LightHeart Foundation, he works with individuals and groups to heal the soul of the world.

He offers sessions and workshops internationally.

Foster is currently working on a new book of prayers and a novel entitled *The Violet Forest: Journey to the Amazon. When Lightning Strikes a Hummingbird* is his first book.